361884

D0708165

LONDON BOROUGH OF GREENWICH

GREENWICH LIBRARIES

RESERVE STOCK (P)

LIB.116

- OCT 1985

John Curry

KEITH MONEY

361884

KEITH MONEY

MICHAEL JOSEPH
LONDON

books by Keith Money

SALUTE THE HORSE
THE EQUESTRIAN WORLD
THE HORSEMAN IN OUR MIDST
THE ART OF THE ROYAL BALLET
THE ART OF MARGOT FONTEYN
THE ROYAL BALLET TODAY
FONTEYN: THE MAKING OF A LEGEND
DANCE DIVERTS

(with Pat Smythe)
FLORIAN'S FARMYARD

(with Peter Beales)
GEORGIAN AND REGENCY ROSES
EARLY VICTORIAN ROSES

in preparation
THE LIFE AND TIMES OF ANNA PAVLOVA
THE OLD ROSE GARDEN

Photographs from page 77 onwards, all © Keith Money who would like to thank Studio Khyber of Watton in Norfolk for equipment and facilities.

First published in Great Britain by Michael Joseph Limited
52 Bedford Square, London WC1B 3EF

© by Keith Money and John Curry 1978

All Rights Reserved. No part of this publication may be reproduced, stored in a retrieval system, or transmitted in any form or by any means, electronic, mechanical, photocopying, recording or otherwise, without the prior permission of the Copyright owners.

ISBN: 0 7181 1653 4

Book designed by Keith Money

Printed in Great Britain by
Beric Press Limited, Crawley
Set in Photina with Vivaldi headings
and Sabon captions by
Filmtype Services Limited, Scarborough
and bound by Hunter & Foulis Limited, Edinburgh

796
910924

BILL AND NELLA STONE

"*Strike forward with the right foot*"
– Capt. T.D. Richardson
(the father of modern
figure-skating)

KEITH MONEY

Introduction

by
Keith Money

John is modest and yet, refreshingly, completely without false modesty. He knew he was good and he knew, also, that he could be better. It took extreme perseverance and courage to pursue the style of skating that he believed in, faced with an indifference, which at times almost amounted to open antagonism, from judging panels that distrusted overt artistic presentation in men's free-skating programmes. His own ideas about this aspect were not fixed by any egomanic stubbornness; they were built steadily on a basic grain of central belief, year after year, until that grain produced the polished result that could no longer be ignored.

His manner on the ice suggests in some measure the man himself: strong, sensitive, open and very likeable. His alertness to nuances of meaning is always apparent but does not produce any edginess of manner; he is calm and philosophical, gaining pleasure from each day and those people he encounters in that day, and perhaps only wistful when he thinks of the long, grey, remorseless haul that brought him to his current position of pre-eminence at the expense of some of the more light-hearted pleasures of adolescence.

His strength is in his character, tempered during these past years to a hard cutting edge that somehow, almost miraculously, remains sheathed. He has the rare ability to balance metaphorically on that thin dividing line between the smooth outer circle of a whirlpool and the annihilating vortex of its centre. The world of Theatre supports him with its expressionist force, but does not claim him with its destructive frenzy of insecurity. If he stopped skating tomorrow, he would find fresh ideas and projects to absorb him. He is a rare performer, and to see him is to know it. I have heard a young girl in a remote village say: 'Oh, I wish he was on television *every* night of the year.' I have heard a rugged colonel exclaim: 'I could go on watching him for hours.' This universal appeal is a hallmark that needs no explaining. We all recognise it, instinctively.

Like countless other people with a generalised interest in sport, I took in skating, as it was presented on television, in small doses. I did not know my toe-loop from my salchow, but when John Curry was on the ice I knew I was looking at blazing talent. His appeal was immediate. We said: 'Look – there's that boy!' long before we knew the name that went with the figure; for John, with his seamless movement and wonderfully expressive arms, produced shapes on the ice that spoke volumes. The execution was clear and apparently effortless, and it was only the commentators' frantic enthusings coupled, almost in the same breath, with hints of potential disaster, that made one worry at all about his progress. Other skaters fell; John seemed to progress through his programmes with a sort of inevitability. That was the impression he gave, even when he himself must have been taut with nerves and doubt.

Perhaps more than anything else, his understanding of music: using it, rather than ignoring it, set him apart from all but a handful of Russian pairs-skaters. To the outsider such as myself, Skating's wilful disregard of musical susceptibility was its abiding fault. I wondered why the average skater bothered with more than a bell or whistle. Within the confines of competition beset by stern and imprisoning convention, John managed to find a programme that satisfied judges looking for technical combinations, while appealing, at the same time, to an audience which was open – as *he* proved – to aesthetic suggestion. We, the audience, usually knew nothing of the earlier compulsory figures, the technical examination that leaves many a skater with crippling scores to be made up in the free-skating programme. We knew only that John Curry had mastered these clinical tasks well, so that he was in strong contention when the free programme came to decide the final results. And it was the free programme that won us viewers immediately, and which won over, ultimately, those chauvinistic judges.

So the artist won the day. John would flinch from the word 'art', as much through conditioning as anything more positive in his reasoning. Of course it is an art, his work, and it is an art that he possesses in extreme measure. With all the competitive awards now garnered by this same art, he feels free to give its expression full rein (and reign) in his own Theatre of Skating. The skill and the daring are there, enhanced by fine music widely chosen, and by noted choreographers intrigued by this man's abilities. I believe that his interpretation of Debussy's *Faune* has a physical distinction that will be remembered and spoken of for generations. In addition, his initial ventures into the field of choreography show, as one would expect, a totally musical awareness coupled with the abiding merits of theatrical clarity and unforced charm. Happily, he has years ahead of him in his seemingly preordained environment, and in his capacity as a performer he sets an awesome example to those who will, inevitably, try to emulate him. They will be following in the wake of a winner who burnished an extra facet to his sport's potential.

The pictures in the opening section of this book come, obviously, from a variety of sources. For the main bulk of the book's illustrations I might, I suppose, have bolstered my credibility as a photographer by posing John in varying representative shapes, enhanced by 'interesting' lighting and pin-sharp clarity, but this would have been to deny him the chance of demonstrating that his remarkable qualities of line and placing are inherent in his every performance; in no way are they an abstract ideal which might not always be achieved in the stress of an actual performance. These pictures are all of John in moments of *skating* (or attending to the peripheral activities of that task) and if they were taken under difficult conditions, that must remain my problem and not his. I used a 35mm camera (a new departure for me) and most of the photographs were taken from the far recesses of auditoria. This is the sort of view seen by a member of the audience. I hope people will study John and his technical perfection – and see less of any photographic imperfections.

The format of this book is similar to one used by me many years ago, on another subject. This method has since gained increasing favour as a way of presenting books on theatrical performers, and I use it again myself in the belief that it remains a valid way of attempting to keep one from getting between the real author (i.e. the subject) and that subject's audience. In most senses this is, therefore, John's book. I have tried to leave intact the idiomatic qualities of John's speech in these transcripts; they are not doctored or reconstructed for any improvement of literary 'style'. As in most things, John expresses himself clearly and honestly. I am aware that some of his own somewhat cryptic humour is not so evident. In talking about the curious and pervading smell of old and decaying ice-rinks, a smell he liked, I commented that he might (in view of the current commercialisation of men's toiletries) have a cologne named after him. '*Eau de Curry*', I said facetiously. 'Mine would be *Eau Dear*!' he shot back immediately, making us both laugh. I recall a lot of laughter in amongst our more serious and analytical discussions. It has been the greatest pleasure, for me, to work with him. He is a perfectionist whose every move is the result of self-critical endeavour; one who has never settled for a *status quo*.

Beginnings

JOSEPH CURRY

My first memory from childhood is a particularly vivid one. My mother was putting me to bed and she had on a yellow, light woollen dress with a very full skirt (it was the fashion just then) and when she turned, the dress swirled out. After that, whenever my mother and father were going out to functions, and were in evening dress, I would always make my mother do a few spins before she left, so that her dress would fly out. I suppose there was something slightly theatrical about the turning.

The first production that I saw in a theatre was *The Desert Song*. I must have seen more versions of *The Desert Song* than anyone else of my generation. My father had a passion for musical comedies and, as I was the only other member of the family who could bear the idea of seeing a musical of any description, it was I who was dragged to them; certainly my two elder brothers never seemed very interested. But I was not really dragged – actually I acquired a taste for them very quickly. We saw everything that came into town: *Annie Get Your Gun, Bless the Bride, The Student Prince, Quaker Girl* – I saw them all. Later, my father started taking me to shows in London, as well as our home city of Birmingham. I loved them and I know that, in some way, I wanted to be a part of it.

At home the only games that I played, and the only toys that I cherished, were to do with the theatre. I devoted myself most to a small model theatre. For this I made the sets and the model characters and even the lights; I did everything. It was typical of me at the time that nothing I did was ever done particularly well, but finally I did come to the decision that I should have a theatre which was properly made. So I made one out of various pieces of wood: a proper structure, with a hardboard covering. I painted it, and got a real curtain that went up and down, and I put proper lights inside it. Best of all, I liked doing the sets and the tiny costumes. Not that I would have done all this in front of anyone else – it was a solitary pursuit. I concocted the little stories that were acted out, and I did a version of *Gulliver's Travels* once. That was very ambitious.

A great event in my life then was the showing of *Aladdin* on television. It was an ice-show, and the star, Jacqueline du Bief, was interviewed during the intermission. She was asked what it took to be a skating champion (she had been World Champion) and she told the interviewer about all the hours of dedication and about how hard one had to try. I do remember she said something to the effect that it was very difficult, even dangerous, to walk on one's toes on the ice, unless one knew how to do it. At moments during the show she did 'ballet' on the toe-picks of her skates, and she said that children should not attempt to do that sort of thing unless they really knew the mechanics of it.

The next ice-shows that I saw were *Humpty Dumpty* and *Glamorous Night*, at the Birmingham Hippodrome. In *Glamorous Night*, one scene was supposedly on the deck of a boat, and when another 'boat' came alongside and fired a shot, the set rocked violently and then began to 'sink'. It was very good! The dancing parts of the musicals certainly appealed to me enormously, but I must admit that I was also very captivated by the singing. Though I broached the subject of dancing lessons to my parents, the answer was a firm 'No'. This did not prevent me from dancing all over the place anyway. I could not even walk up a flight of stairs normally; I would always do something like two up, one down, then three up and a skip and a hop. I did this all over the house as well as in the garden. I never knew why I did it; I just could not stop myself. Sometimes I still catch myself doing it!

At school I was always good at athletics; I seemed to win everything. I ran faster, and jumped higher and further, than most of the others. Principally, I think, because I was well coordinated. Although I did well at Physical Training, I was absolutely lousy at football or cricket; but when I saw the ice-show on television I thought that was perfect, and I said immediately: 'I want to go skating.' Somewhat to my surprise, my mother said: 'Yes, that's fine.' Skating, being a sport, was approved of, whereas the dancing idea had been treated with grave mistrust.

The decision concerning skating came as something of a relief. At that time, my father and my middle brother were both suffering from tuberculosis but were not actually in a nursing home, they were accommodated in the house. We lived in Acocks Green, a suburb of Birmingham, and although we had a fairly large house, it did mean that part of it was essentially a nursing unit, and all that part I was not allowed to visit. Even so, we were constantly shot full of innoculations, and had also to go off every few months for full medical check-ups. Because of all this it was very difficult for my mother to find the time to take me skating, but eventually she managed it – I think around the time of my seventh birthday, in September. I still remember the occasion with crystal clarity. When I walked in, the first thing that hit me was the smell. It was a pervading smell that forms part of all those early memories and it is like nothing else; all old ice-rinks used to have the same smell. It was an odour comprised of damp wood, damp cold air, coconut matting and some sort of ammonia – unlike any other concoction one could imagine. And I liked it. Describing its components makes it sound anything but pleasant, but for me it was wonderful and I felt absolutely 'at home' with that smell.

My first initiation into the famous smell was at the old Summerhill Ice Rink, which has now been demolished. It was a 25-minute drive from our home, and in those days it had an old-world style about it, with a proper commissionaire, wearing a very smart uniform, standing at the door. Once inside, the first thing my mother did was to go over to the desk where the lessons were booked. There was a list of the teachers, written on the wall and, next to their names, the various prices. Some charged six shillings – the top price for a fifteen-minute lesson – and the lowest charge was perhaps two shillings and sixpence. My mother did not choose the most expensive and she did not choose the least expensive; she chose somewhere nearer the middle, a three-shilling lesson, and that teacher happened to be Ken Vickers.

Now this was really extraordinary luck, because here was a man who not only knew and understood the real basics of skating; he had also a very marked sense of style. In fact he was one of the most correct style-skaters I have ever seen in my life, with a back just like a ramrod, very correct, and perfectly 'placed'. When I first set eyes on him I thought merely that he was very upright and straight, but if I think about it now, I realise how beautifully he skated.

So it was Ken Vickers who took me into the skate shop on that first occasion, and there he fitted a correct pair of boots on me, and my mother then bought them. With the boots on, I was told to go to a corner of the ice-rink and wait at the top of the stairs until he came to take me onto the ice. At that rink, there were four or five steps down to the ice. When he arrived I clomped down the steps and then, literally the very first time I put skates onto ice, I had a teacher, Ken Vickers, holding my hand. The first thing he said was: 'Put your feet together and stand up straight.' The next thing he told me to do was to bend my knees and keep my back up. That is just about the best advice one can give to any skater, no matter what they are doing. Bend the knees and keep the back straight! So I went along for about twenty feet, with one hand on the barrier and the other hand held by him, and then I said: 'No, I don't need to hold your hand; I can do it by myself.' And I could. I went off, skating around quite naturally.

After that first lesson, because my mother's time was so limited, I used to go in, have my fifteen minutes of teaching and then, just as I was really getting things going, I would be pulled off the ice and taken home again. But it was all for the best, because I was never given any time, in those early years, to 'roughhouse' around and acquire the bad habits that most skaters pick up from too much early freedom on the ice. I always looked forward to the skating lessons tremendously. At that time I did not go to school on Wednesday afternoon, which was our afternoon off, and my mother always took me to skate then; she was very good about keeping it going.

I soon began to notice, after the first few lessons, that my teacher would go over and have a chat with my mother, and they would stand and talk and 'look' in my direction. It seems that he did in fact tell her, after those initial excursions, that I had a definite talent of some sort and that I should, as a result, be made to work hard at it. Actually, there was no danger of my not working hard; I used to get irritated by the sight of other people skating really proficiently.

The competitive element in skating crept up on me without my being aware of it. All skaters are really trained to compete; it is not something that trainers even consult their pupils about. My initiation was rather surreptitious. I was taken along to the ice-rink one Saturday morning, as opposed to the usual Wednesday ventures, and when we got there, my teacher said to me: 'Now, there are going to be a few people around watching, but don't take any notice of them because they are nothing to do with you. All *you* have to do is go out, do a spiral and a three-jump and a spin, and then stop and come off. Just stop and come straight off.'

My mother had given me a new sweater so I had that on, and I went out and did the steps, which were all fine, and then I came off the ice. A lot of other people then went out, and they did the same sort of things that I had done. Then everything stopped and, after about ten minutes, somebody came along and told me I had won a competition! They gave me a cup, much to the annoyance of a little girl, in a new frilly frock, who came second. She had been there to win, and there was a crying temper over the result. I can still remember her name! The competition was called The Hop, Skip and Jump, and I was between seven and eight years old.

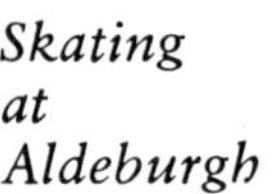

Skating at Aldeburgh

In those early years we went once to Aldeburgh, in Suffolk, for the Christmas holidays. We had been told, before we went, that sometimes the mere froze at that time of year, so I took my skates with me, hoping that it would. And sure enough it did. I think I was the only child with skates, so I was able to whizz around, showing off. It was like heaven to me; I had never seen so much ice.

But I was also a bit afraid, and would not venture out very far from the edge. My father had always told me awful stories about people falling through ice. He used to say that the ice did not break and make a hole through which one fell; what really happened was that it broke in a section and then turned like a revolving door and shut one in underneath. Perhaps this really does happen; I do not know. But according to my father, the poor victim would be swimming around underneath, looking for the hole through which he had fallen, and of course there would be no hole. I think he told me all this to prevent my going out on a pond alone. Whenever there was any really cold weather, I liked to go and skate outdoors. I skated at Cannon Hill Park and various other places in Birmingham. Even the Walsall Arboretum. But I am still afraid to skate above deep water because of this lingering image of the revolving door swallowing one up, leaving one looking through from the other side.

Soon there were lots of competitions; usually slightly more advanced ones. I knew exactly what competitions were and I thought it was nice to be given things that looked like fancy egg-cups. My brothers, at school, had won events on Sports Days and had always been presented with small cups, but if *I* won things at school I was given match-box toys; they always gave the 'babies' miniature cars or lorries. I hated all that. I wanted a medal or a cup like the older boys. I once made such a fuss that my father had one of the toys mounted on a plinth. It really did seem terrible to me that everyone else who won the hundred yards got a cup or a medal, whereas all I got for winning the hundred yards was a tractor.

So at last, by skating, I began to get egg-cups to go with all the little match-box toys. I got so many of them that it became rather a penance for my mother, who was left with the job of keeping them clean. I liked winning, principally because I disliked losing.

MORRIS STUDIOS

EVERARD STUDIO

'Programmes' were an absolute mystery to me then. In skating, teachers make up routines and set them to selections of bits of music, and these individual routines are known as programmes. One day, another boy came up to me and said: 'Let's do our programmes', and I, not wanting to appear ignorant, covered up by saying: 'Oh, all right. You do yours first.' So off he went and proceeded to do all his little jumps and spins, and it all seemed very ordinary to me – just the usual jumps and spins, so I then went off and did a whole lot of jumps and spins too. And when I had finished, the boy said: 'What music do you do it to?' and I said, lying glibly: 'I don't know the name of it', because in fact I had never had a programme made for me. After that, I went to my teacher and said: 'Why haven't I got a programme?' To which he replied: 'Because you're not ready to do one yet.'

Eventually I did get a programme, which was to *The Village Swallows* by Strauss. It had in the sound-track of the record what were supposed to be birds – in all probability musicians rubbing corks against wet bottles; all twittering away. And this was the piece to which my teacher set my first programme. As a child I used to do a very reasonable arabesque, quite naturally. (It went much higher up, then, than it does now!) So my teacher made use of this, setting an arabesque one way, and then one the other way, and a small jump and a spin – that was about it. Then I heard the music. Well! Instead of doing it all the way my teacher had shown me, when I came to the arabesques I fluttered my hands – like birds! And when I did the jumps, I reached up into the air with my hands and made more little fluttering wings! It really did seem to me at the time that as there were all those birds singing I might as well make use of them. In my first competitions with the music, all the other boys were technically so much better than me. But *I* had the birdsong! And

I used to *win*, much to everyone else's annoyance. Afterwards, they would say: 'But you haven't done your axel. *I* did an axel, and *you* won! This isn't fair!'

It did not take me long to find out that if I skated in time with the music, which was a perfectly natural thing for me to do (it just 'happened'), and if I did my little 'movements', then the judges would usually say: 'That was very good; we liked that.' And I would win. But the other boys were always extremely upset.

There were a few times when I skated in competitions and was beaten by children of a very low standard – I had got nervous suddenly, and had fallen all over the place. Then, I felt really terrible. Like everybody, I went through a period when I would be going marvellously in the practice and the warm-up, and everyone would say: 'Oh well, there's no question of who's going to win', and then I would go out and fall down flat on my face. I remember one competition in London, at Wembley, when I fell over six times in three minutes. I simply could not stand up; it was as if I had no skates on. I came off the ice and had not the slightest clue as to what was happening. When I was about eleven or twelve I had a phase of disasters, but usually I would skate fairly well.

The most embarrassing thing I ever did was during a skating competition at the Queen's Ice Rink, on the first occasion that I had travelled down to take part in the Queen's Cup. I performed the first part of a school figure and then simply left, quite in a dream. I skated one-and-a-half circles, and then – simply glided off the ice! I remember my teacher of the time, a lady, ran right out of the building, and all the judges came up and said: 'What on earth happened?' And I replied: 'I'm awfully sorry. I don't know really why I did it.' Nor did I know.

EVERARD STUDIO

Skating in Birmingham

Holidaying in Penzance, with brothers Michael and Andrew

QUEENIE SIMPSON

EVERARD STUDIO

E. RICHARDSON

Trafalgar Day, Birmingham 1965

with Mother and Andrew

Until I was twelve, there was no conflict between my schooling and my skating. At home I got on well with my family, and at school I kept up with everyone else in the class. But stresses in family life can seem magnified for any child, and I was no different in this respect. As things became more earnest at home, so I became more and more determined about what I really wanted to do with my time. My father's illnesses created a pressure from which skating was, for me at any rate, an escape. Once at the rink, I rather dreaded going home again. At the rink I was in an environment where I could forget completely everything else. In skating I was happy. Along with my fantasy games, the skating was an escape which, when I went to a boarding school for eighteen months, I found I could dispense with; I did not miss it at all. Perhaps I did create a substitute at that school: I was always being teased for 'dancing about'. But I liked the school and I had no desire for the holidays to hasten along. When I did find myself at home, skating suddenly seemed very important again.

After four difficult years, when I was sixteen, my father died. He had seen me skate twice.

EVERARD STUDIO

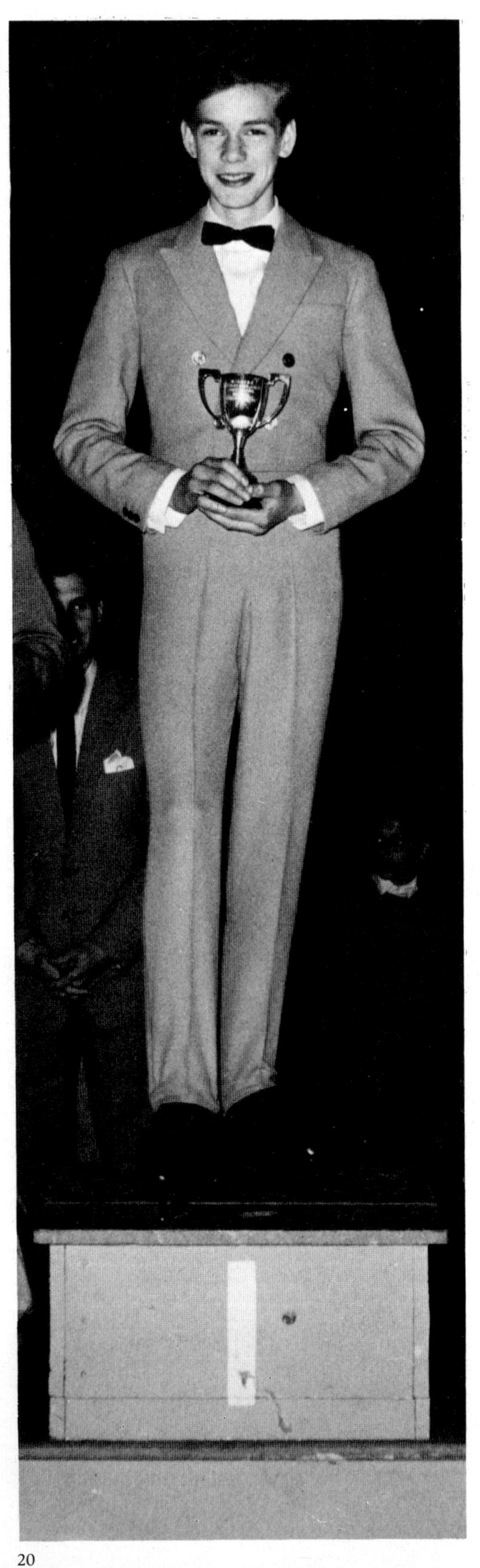

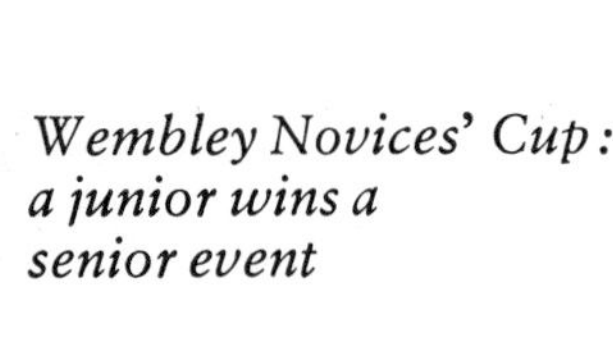

Wembley Novices' Cup: a junior wins a senior event

JAN V.A

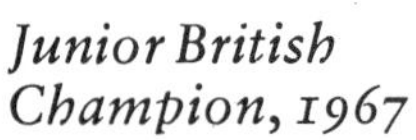

Junior British Champion, 1967

JAN V.A.

1968, the Jennings Trophy for free-skating, at Nottingham Ice Stadium

R. SILVESTER

First win in the British Men's Skating Championship, 1970

Grey Days

After my father's death, my schooling continued for a time solely with a tutor, whom I had inherited from my brother. My tutor hated the arrangement as much as I did; it was a mutual loathing. I think he was very glad to see the end of me and my grubby exercise books when the situation was finally terminated. By then we had suddenly found ourselves in very reduced financial circumstances and the tutoring went, along with other 'luxuries'. It seemed a watershed in my life and as I was stubbornly resolved to pursue skating as a career, London beckoned. It was a symbol of independence. I had failed, in the past, to make my parents accept skating as a tolerable way of earning a living; they had both remained unconvinced, either about its possible financial rewards from performing or ultimate teaching, or indeed about its social 'suitability'. My ambition probably seemed rather perverse; it was certainly assumed that the phase was an infatuation that would pass, leaving me with nothing in its place. I realised that if I was to prove my point I should strike out from home.

My first plan on reaching London was to skate under the tutelage of Armand Perrin in Streatham. He was a Swiss coach who had taught in Brighton prior to London, and a few weeks after my arrival he moved again – ironically, to a new ice-rink at Solihull, very close to our address in Birmingham. So back I went, home again. I was taught by Mr Perrin for six months until I had advanced to the stage where London beckoned again – this time in the form of Richmond and Arnold Gerschwiler. I managed to find 'digs' in Richmond, and to pay for them and the lessons, I got a job in a small family-style supermarket. I was quite good at arranging the cut meats artistically; it was the nearest I came to them, with my salary!

In Birmingham, my father's firm, which did light precision engineering, had made component parts for the National Cash Register Company in London, and through a contact I next acquired a post with them at their offices in Marylebone Road. The job was as a receptionist of sorts: ushering in clients, arranging demonstration time-tables

with Armand Perrin at a senior International event in Prague, 1968

sightseeing in London

HEINZ WIRZ

and generally trying to look as if I was awake. This last was the most difficult aspect of the job. The firm was very understanding about my skating commitments and arranged my employment for an afternoon schedule, from two o'clock until five. This gave me the morning free in Richmond, where I got up at five each morning and then trained at the rink until twelve. The first two years with Mr Gerschwiler were very exciting ones. As the trainer of Sjoukje Dijkstra and Aja Vrzanova, Mr Gerschwiler was considered one of the world's foremost teachers of the technique of school figures in skating. On the other hand, his free-skating pupils were not distinguished, and so it may have been pleasant for him to have, in me, a pupil who was not always falling over. At any event we seemed to get on very well for the first two years, and certainly my school figures began to improve under his coaching.

Mr Gerschwiler's schedule in those days included a winter season in Davos, from December through to March. For the first two years I could not afford to take part in those winter seasons; it was all way beyond my means. For the third winter season it became imperative that I should go with him to Davos, as I was due to skate in the European Championships that year, having done well in the British Championships; so, somehow, I got myself to Davos. How I hated it! The cold seemed unbearable. Mr Gerschwiler's timetable paid no heed to comfort. Although the ice-rink was there all day, he insisted that we be on it at seven in the morning. This, in an alpine resort in January, is before the sun makes any impact on the scene. It was so cold that often, when one inhaled, one's nostrils sealed themselves together. If I blew my nose and then put the handkerchief back in my pocket, when I next came to need it I would find that the damp cloth had frozen itself to my leg, inside my trousers. For me, the unpleasantness of the conditions was something with which I could not cope, with the result that my figure-skating did not merely deteriorate, it fell apart. I was demoralised by my inability to rise above the bad conditions which included, as well as the cold, uneven ice. Because I seemed incapable of surmounting these various challenges, Mr Gerschwiler and I began to have terrible arguments. I must have been a total misery, that first year in Davos.

By the time of my second visit a year later, I had hit on some sort of solution to my impending unhappiness with the place.

I painted a rosy picture of Davos to all my friends in England, persuading them to invest in winter holidays there. With this sort of manoeuvring I thus masterminded a succession of friends arriving for a week or two at a time throughout the entire period. I battled with the elements on the ice all morning and until about four in the afternoon, then went off with my friends and indulged in tobogganing and snow-fights – all the things that are fun to do and which are strictly forbidden to ice-skaters in training. The fun that I was having by trailing to the top of the mountain and then plunging down the toboggan run every evening was not, I suppose, something calculated to endear myself to my trainer, and perhaps my school figures really did suffer, but sometimes conditions were against us all – even the most noted skaters there found the ice impossible. There was a period when it never stopped snowing and the effect was hopelessly demoralising. It is difficult enough to do school figures in perfect conditions, but to attempt them in a wind, with an inch-and-a-half of snow on the ice and more being added by the minute – that does not boost one's morale. Even if one completed a circle without being blown backwards at the halfway stage, one would look back only to see somethink like a mouse-trail in the snow. We went round and round, doggedly following those 'mouse-trails' in the snow and feeling, all the while, as if we were freezing to death. We descended from the snowy wastes to Lyon for the World Championships in 1971, and none of us who had been in Davos did as well as we should have done. By then, the International Skating Union had decreed that no World or European Championships should be held in outdoor arenas, so our mouse-trails in the snow were a distinct contrast to the untroubled perfection of an indoor rink such as Lyon. Our weaknesses became glaringly apparent. If there had still been some chance of encountering bad skating conditions at the World Championships, then our battling with the elements on 'Bald Mountain' might have served us in good stead. As it was, the certainty of conditions in an indoor rink negated any outdoor training. I think it was really the cold that froze my rapport with Mr Gerschwiler, but by the end of that winter we could not look at one another. The World Championships at Lyon marked the end of my training under him.

The National Cash Register Company was very good about holding my job open for me while I went away to compete at the various European fixtures. Back in the Accounting Machine Showroom, on the first floor, I would once more usher the clients to their seats and try to co-ordinate the various demonstrations and, eventually, even operate the machines myself. I did this with parrot-fashion learning; not with any understanding of the internal intricacies. This mimicking of other's skills even progressed me to the point of operating a computer that worked on telephonic input. I could do it, but I never understood it. Once the doors closed at five I would go back to Richmond on the tube-train, invariably fast asleep. Thinking back on it, that period of my life is the epitome of everything that I never want to happen to me again. My landlady was very kind to me, but with no money there was no freedom. Eventually I progressed to a bed-sitter, and this was a slightly more liberating experience. Even so, the cold seemed ever-present; there was never a shilling for the gas meter, and stepping out of bed onto a cold floor, then washing in the cold, then going to a cold ice-rink at six in the morning all seemed unrelievedly horrible. But skating still exercised its hold over me. I could never contemplate the idea of a full-time career selling cash registers, but there were times when I considered the possibility of joining *Holiday on Ice*, particularly after a disastrous season such as surrounded the World Championships at Lyon. However, to be told by the owner of the show that I would never be any good, that I would never beat anyone in competitive skating and that therefore I might as well accept his offer for a season in *Holiday on Ice*; this was sufficient to make me more determined than ever. Back I would go to the chill of the bed-sitter and the ice-rink.

At the age of twenty I went to America for the first time. Being my usual impoverished self I was at a loss how to get myself to a teacher by the name of Peter Dunfield, whose modern attitudes to teaching had intrigued me at the Championships in Lyon. I asked my close friend Penny Malec what one did when one wanted money. She pointed out that the safest method, if least likely, was to approach a bank. So, without any hope of success, I asked my bank manager if my usual sixteen shillings and eightpence account could be extended to accommodate a four hundred pound overdraft. I explained that the four hundred pounds (added to a three hundred pound loan from a friend) was the absolute minimum needed for the summer season of training that had been tentatively mapped out for me with Peter Dunfield. I was dumbfounded when the bank manager agreed; I could not believe it. He

NANCY STREETER

Liberty

knew how little I was earning and I have never really understood why he took the risk; it was not as if he was due for retirement! Thanks to him, I found myself on a charter flight to the United States.
I arrived at that time of the year when New York is like a kettle about to blow its lid. Life was full of extremes. I had already written to say that I could not contemplate the season unless there was reasonable accommodation arranged for me; I could not face an American version of my bed-sitter. Peter Dunfield arranged that I should, therefore, stay with some people called Frank and Nancy Streeter.

For once in my life I really landed on my feet with a bang, for I was taken into one of the nicest homes I had ever been in, with the most tranquil home atmosphere that I had experienced, with people who were interesting, and really interested in all the things that I liked. They made my time there as comfortable as one could ever hope for; they became, happily, treasured friends in my life. There was only one cloud in the summer sky: Peter Dunfield and John Curry did not establish any vestige of a teacher-pupil relationship; we did not get along at all!

I spent the first six weeks of the summer season in New York, and the second six weeks were supposed to be spent in Toronto. In Canada, my skating seemed to be getting worse by the minute; it literally reduced me to floods of tears. Mr Dunfield had started by telling me that I was far too old to learn anything; there seemed to be an American belief that something not learned at three weeks of age was something that would never be learned. Some of the harsh comments were not easily borne when I thought of the four hundred pounds that had purchased them. One morning I went down to the ice-rink early, at six o'clock. There,

in Central Park, with the Streeter family

I set out all my Gold figures – all the ones that must be executed in a World Championship; the whole syllabus. The figures that I set out that morning in Toronto were so awful that they would not have gained me a pass in a Silver test. For two hours, all over the ice, I set out terrible, miserable figures. I looked at them and thought: 'This is ridiculous. You are away from home and you don't like it here. You are homesick. What are you *doing* here?' At eight in the morning I was back at my accommodation, telephoning the charter flight company. When was the next flight to England? It transpired that my ticket was valid for a flight due to leave in three hours, or not until another ten days. I confirmed for the flight in three hours and in half that time I was packed and at the airport. Before I knew it, I was back in England. It was one of two occasions in my life when I acted with total precipitation.

Homesick, I decided to try Birmingham again. The house was empty and locked when I arrived, but I found the key where my mother had hidden it and I let myself in. For the next three days I sat inside the empty house, until my mother returned. She was astonished to find me there. The mental turmoil, coupled with three days' lack of food, emptied my reserves, and for several weeks I remained at home at a very low ebb.

Eventually, I took myself back to London to try again. There, Alison Smith opened up her heart and her home to me. She had been a pupil of Mr Gerschwiler and had subsequently become a teacher at the rink in Richmond, which Mr Gerschwiler controlled; she had become a good friend to me. Now, when I asked her if she would consider taking me as a pupil, she readily agreed. When Mr Gerschwiler found out, he called her to his office and said: 'Do you really think you can teach this boy?' Alison replied that she did not know whether she could or not, but she thought there was a possibility and so she said that she would try. It was the first time that a pupil at that rink had transferred teachers, and Alison's decision was not warmly greeted. I had, after all, been thought of as one of the more promising pupils, despite the current view of my potentiality. From that time, it seemed to Alison and to

OTTO MEIJEUR

New York: a Briton turning out in the rain

with Alison Smith, waiting for the marks to come up

me that normal levels of internal co-operation and goodwill at the rink had disappeared. It got to the point where both of us dreaded an impending training session. At five-thirty in the morning, spirits were always at a very low ebb. On some mornings Alison would say: 'I simply cannot face going in there today.' At other times it would be me voicing the same feeling. I could never understand why other teachers managed to get in my way so much. I could find no reason for other people shouting at us. We worked on, becoming tighter and tighter, controlling ourselves.

It seems, in looking back on that period, that I spent most of my time while skating in England holding on to my temper; ninety per cent of my energy seemed to be spent that way. I never did lose my temper. I knew that if I did, I would lose the day with it. That we both would lose. For a year or so I begged Alison to leave; to go anywhere in the world. Any rink in the world would have welcomed her excellence in teaching skills. At that time, she decided to stay on, but later she did leave. Now, she no longer teaches in England. The country has lost one of its best teachers. She felt compelled to leave, just as I felt compelled to leave. I wished for the facilities that were in London, but those facilities did not appear to be entirely open to me personally. I was made to feel that I had chosen the wrong teacher. Whatever the basis of fact, the feeling was potent enough to make me view my trips to America with increasing relief. These trips were made possible in an entirely fortuitous way.

Under Alison's guidance I had come fourth in the World Championships at Bratislava in 1972. Immediately after the performance, I had been backstage with Alison, as usual gibbering at her: 'Was it all right? Was it all right?' when a man walked up to me and said: 'My name is Ed Mosler. Your skating has given me a great deal of pleasure over the last three years and I'd like to help you.' Thinking that he was there to offer some friendly criticism, I said merely: 'Thank you very much; that's very nice of you', and I walked away. He came after me and said: 'No – you don't understand. I'm with the American team and I'd like to help you.' I still thought he was wanting to tell me why I did not jump higher, or do this or that thing better, so I said: 'Thank you' again, and was turning to leave, when he said: 'I'd like to talk to you later at the hotel', to which I replied in what must have seemed a very off-hand manner: 'Oh, all right; maybe later, when we get home.'

The following day the same man walked up to me, laughed, and said: 'You don't really know who I am, do you?' and I had to admit that I did not. He explained to me that he was the man who had sponsored most, if not all, of the American ice-skaters and that he had a policy and a Foundation that allowed him to sponsor only Americans, but that he had so enjoyed my skating that he wanted to make a special exception and sponsor me. And he added: 'Would five hundred pounds help?' At that time, five hundred pounds was like a two-year assurance for me. As it turned out, the result of a ten-minute talk was that I was removed from the ranks of the 'broke' to a position where finance was no longer of any overriding concern. I was in a state of complete and utter shock at this turn of events. I went up to the tiny hotel bedroom in Bratislava, and in that room, which I was sharing with another skater, I paced up and down in the gap beside the two beds, which were jammed head to head and which took up most of the space in the room. Up and down I walked, for hours. For so long, the consideration of shillings and pence had ruled every aspect of my day to day existence; the sudden possibility of that worry being removed, at a stroke, left me rather dazed.

Back in London, two days passed and then through the door fluttered a letter from Mr Mosler, confirming his intention and asking how it could best be effected. I got in touch with the National Skating Association, a body which had, for four years, made murmurings about finding me a sponsor. I told them I now had sponsorship offered to me and I asked them, as a matter of form, for approval. The next shock to my system was the fact that there was some question as to whether I should accept the offer because it was from an American! There was some feeling that it might be better if I went on the way I had been going, skating on cornflakes, rather than actually accepting money from an American. I argued strongly against this theory, and as a result an enormous problem vanished suddenly from my life. I battled on after that for one more year at Richmond, slightly cushioned by the feeling of independence given by the financial security.

Still with Alison, I went to the European Championships at Zagreb and skated well, coming third. The World Championships followed at Munich. I felt I was set for an advancement in the competition, having come fourth the previous year and having done so well at Zagreb. I skated abysmally. It is the only time in my life when I can say, without fear of any contradiction, that my skating was bad;

totally bad. My nerves had taken over. I could hardly move: I was paralysed with fear. As as result I dropped four places on my results of the previous year. For twelve months I had spent Mr Mosler's money, and that thought contributed greatly to my mortification. In skating one is up or one is down, and down is to be nowhere. The judges came to me unanimously and told me that I must give up, because no one who dropped from fourth to seventh could ever improve. I went to Mr Mosler and told him how mortified I was by my performance, and I explained that I could not go on accepting any more of his money. Mr Mosler, in his characteristic way, said: 'Well, there were a few moments in that programme that *I* thought were exceptionally beautiful.' My reaction was that there could not have been one-thousandth of a second that was all right, but Mr Mosler insisted that there were a few moments, which he described as some of the most beautiful skating he had ever seen. Unconvinced, I told him that I was sorry that I had wasted his money, that I could not accept any more of it, and that I was going to give up. He said: 'Well, I'm not going to tell you not to; what I am going to tell you is to wait a few weeks and think about it. Because I think you should not give up.' So I waited – for three months.

Staying with the Streeters in New York during that time, I thought about the decision constantly, depressed for all of those three months. And at the end of that time, I came to the decision that I was not going out of Skating through the back door; that even if I came only sixth, I was going to prove to myself that I could do a decent World Championship. I was going to make changes. I was going to put right everything that everyone said was wrong with my skating, and to start this process I was going to take myself to Slavka Kahout, who was the trainer of Janet Lynn, and marvellous at her job. I determined to ask her to teach me. If she said 'No', I would stop, but if she would agree, then I felt that she could construct for me a beautiful programme that would give me my confidence.

Slavka Kahout had at that time been married for only a short time and was expecting her first child. Naturally, she was in no mood to take on another skater; she was really in the process of dropping all her teaching commitments. I spent much of one afternoon explaining to her what it was that I wanted to do and how much it meant to me that she should be my teacher. She sat and listened, and for about an hour said nothing. I do not think she even looked at me; she has a rather unnerving way of not looking at people! Finally, she told me that she could not teach me; that she was happily married and that there was thus a whole new side of her life that she had not experienced before. She was not going to allow anything to intrude upon this state. 'But if I were you, this is what I would do. . . .' And with that, she outlined for me a nine-months' training plan involving two teachers: one called Gus Lussi, the other called Carlo Fassi. She told me I should go for six weeks – no more than six weeks – to Gus Lussi, and during that time I should not even take my figure skates with me; that I should just free-skate and jump and jump until I had learned as much as I could from Gus Lussi, who was really the inventor of modern jumping. 'Don't even think about school figures. Forget them. Don't do them at all. And when you are absolutely sick of jumping, jump a bit more. And then, go to Colorado, to Carlo Fassi. And take your figure skates with you. And then do figures until they are coming out of your eyeballs. And when you cannot look at another circle, go and do another two hours.'

I had met Gus Lussi once and had not felt any particular liking for him; and on the occasion when I had met Carlo Fassi he had terrified the wits out of me. This had been at a World Championships, when he had been so involved in his work that he had had very little time for surface pleasantries. As a result, the few words that he did utter to me were sharp to a degree. But because it was Slavka suggesting these things, I thought: 'Okay, I'll do it.' I wrote very polite letters to both gentlemen and was amazed to receive by return post an acceptance from both. Yes, they would make space for me and yes, I could join whenever I wanted. Perhaps Slavka had spoken to them.

My initial training with Gus Lussi was bewildering. Here was the world's greatest jump-teacher, and the ice he began teaching me on was no larger than an average sitting-room. On the first day, I found myself in a tiny area separated off from an enormous, Olympic-sized ice-rink. As every minute passed, I expected Gus Lussi to step out onto the main area of that rink at Lake Placid. But he did not; we started there – on a piece of ice twenty feet by thirty feet. Triple jumps on a piece of ice I could not have fitted a school figure onto; what trick was this? There began then, on that portion of ice, a most drastic dis-assembling of everything that I had been taught. I fell, badly, on an average of thirty or forty times a day. My embarrassment knew no bounds. There I was, supposedly one of the best skaters in the world, and all that anybody saw of me was an endless series of slides across the ice, ending – all too soon in that confined space – in a heap crumpled against the barrier. Nearby were ten-year-old girls flying around, doing things which seemed beyond the person who was a European medallist and British Champion! I fell, and I fell, and I fell. There came a point, after three weeks, when I could not do even an axel – the most simple of the rotation jumps. Even *that* was beyond me. I despaired. The

NORDISK PRESSEFOTO

third in the European Championships, Zagreb 1974; with Alison Smith and team leader Eileen Anderson

evenings, away from the rink, were spent in abject misery thinking about the misery on the rink.

And then, after three weeks, the tide changed. It suddenly clicked: what that man was trying to tell me. And occasionally a jump would work. Not only did it work, but I sensed I was doing it better than I would have done it before, with more elevation and more 'air' in the jump; much better in general. I had been told so often by people there: 'You're twenty-three. You're too old. You'll *never* do it!' And now all those people who had giggled at me began giggling less and looking more. I was no longer told that at my age it was impossible to change. I *had* changed. Mr Lussi's trick had worked. His theory had been that everybody jumping on ice normally relies on momentum, and that at forty miles an hour even the most earth-bound mortal must achieve some sort of elevation. But in a confined space,

with judge Sally Ann Stapleford at the rinkside in Copenhagen

arriving in Copenhagen for the European Championships 1975; ultimately placed second

one has no momentum and is therefore dependent upon achieving height by one's own muscular co-ordination.

I took my new-found technique to Spain, for six weeks with Alison, and Alison seemed very pleased with what she found. With my figure skates once more in my bag, I headed next for Colorado, to join the great Carlo Fassi.

NORDISK PRESSEFOTO

During the time when first I began to compete abroad regularly, I felt more and more that ice-skaters' costumes were extremely dull. They seemed to follow the style set in previous years, with no concessions to natural evolution or adaptation. The one style from the commercial clothing industry which did make an impact, that of bell-bottomed trousers, happened to be the one that was least suitable for a skater's physical line. It accentuated the feet and truncated the line of the legs. Although there are so many unwritten regulations in competition skating, there are no explicit rules concerning costumes, with the exception of the obvious one guarding against any blatant hint of indecency – a charge unlikely to have been levelled against the men in the days of my early competitions, where we all dressed in baggy trousers, shirt with tie, and the ubiquitous monkey-jacket on top of all that. If all we hear about Nijinsky's final appearance in St Petersburg is as it has been reported, then it is almost certain that the Imperial Family of that time would still not have approved of men's skating costumes of the immediate past era, where high-speed athleticism was performed in a variety of ill-fitting trousers and underpants. It was as if the dance-belt had never been marketed.

For myself, I was concerned to find a way of wearing a costume that would combine some sort of visual harmony with the musical content, while at the same time demonstrating a good 'line'. At Bratislava in 1973 I experimented with black pants, black velvet tunic and a cream silk shirt, the effect suggested by the male dancer's costume in traditional versions of the ballet *Les Sylphides*. Although this outfit drew comment, the reaction was in no way adverse. I next experimented with navy-blue trousers and a navy-blue leotard or plain roll-necked sweater, with no additional decoration whatsoever. This outfit allowed me full freedom of movement and was, as far as I was concerned, totally suited to my task, but onlookers began to speak of my casual and 'under-dressed' appearance, as if I was still in practice costume.

SEPP SCHONMETZLER

I decided to try something different again. Part of Stravinsky's *The Rite of Spring* appealed to me as the basis of a short free-skating programme, being particularly dramatic and intense. I designed a costume for this brief programme: a blue leotard and pants over-painted with a 'vapour trail' of white that began at one wrist and wound down around the body to the hip. In any kind of turn there was, as a result, a strong visual emphasis on the spiral. I wore this costume at the European Championships at Copenhagen in 1975. I was in strong contention after the school figures section; then came my *Rite of Spring* programme. After that phase of the competition, in which I skated well, I was told by officials of the ISU that I must not wear the costume again as it had influenced the judges against me. The form-fitting line, which was entirely innocuous (*see left*), had startled them. It seems they were less startled by other men wearing sequins, spangles and nylon lace sleeves, then the vogue in men's skating competitions.

I reverted to plain blue or black after this, and no doubt looked under-dressed again. But coincidentally, my competition marks went up again thereafter. I did the same *Rite of Spring* programme, at the same technical level, a few weeks after wearing the 'notorious spiral'. This was at the World Championships in Colorado, and in that section I beat not only my fellow European competitors but also those from the rest of the world.

Good old navy-blue!

Happy Days

I walked into the rink at Denver one morning, very hot and very tired after a three-day drive that had seemed endless. It would be no more than the truth to say that at that time I did not like Mr Fassi and Mr Fassi did not like me. We shook hands without either of us smiling. Mr Fassi made basic pleasantries about my journey and then I departed to settle in. After a few days, I think Mr Fassi realised that I was not the monster he thought I was, and I began to realise that he was not the monster that *I* had thought *he* was! We got along together; in fact we soon enjoyed each other's company. I can say now that, in my experience, Mr Fassi is the best trainer in the world, not only because he knows the technique of skating inside out and backwards, but also because he knows how to prepare a person for a competition. This is an art, and one that eludes most teachers, who can teach one how to do something, but not how to do it in a competition. Mr Fassi can do that. Everybody thinks that the Italian background makes him temperamental. He *is* very bubbly and full of spirit, and yet he is the most consistent teacher one could find; his temperament is totally even. He does not have days when he arrives feeling bad, making everyone else suffer for that; he does not have days when he is in such a good mood that one mistrusts him for that reason; one can rely totally on the evenness of his mood. And Mrs Fassi! I was completely bowled over by the lovely Mrs Fassi. Mrs Fassi is German; very methodical and very precise.

I was taught by Mr Fassi and Mrs Fassi – a system which worked well at competitions in particular, for if Mr Fassi had to be with Dorothy Hamill or one of the other skaters, Mrs Fassi could be with me. Of all the pupils, I suspect I was the one with whom Mrs Fassi got on best, but this did not prevent her being a stern taskmaster. Sometimes, on the ice, Mr Fassi would look at something I had done, and say: 'This is a really hexellent figure! Hexellent; hexellent!' And invariably Mrs Fassi would then

Left: exhibition performance at Sun Valley, Idaho

say something like: 'Oh – no, no. Just look down here. There's a slight double line; just here. Look, Carlo!' I could not get past her with anything; she was wonderful. If it was a really good figure, she might say: 'Oh, it was pretty good; pretty good.' And we got on like the proverbial house on fire, Mr Fassi and Mrs Fassi and I; no problems. I suspect Mr Fassi thinks I am the easiest person he has taught because I am fairly well disciplined; I do not have days when I say I cannot do things; I just plod on.

The time in Denver was an ecstatically happy one for me. The rink was first-class; Mr and Mrs Fassi were marvellous, and I had friends there: Dr and Mrs Graham had an apartment very close to mine and I would often take their two children out on various expeditions. The climate there is splendid, with long summers, hot and dry but not unpleasant, and winters which are cold, brilliant and sunny. I started to feel marvellously alive, as well as happy. Skating could not have seemed easier. The most difficult part of the day was in washing and getting dressed, so perfectly was the rest of it arranged for me; everything where I wanted it when I needed it. Perfect ice, and Mr Fassi always in the same mood; a half-wit could have done it. All I had to do was skate, and for perhaps the first and only time in my life, skating was absolutely easy for me. Even in New York it had never been so easy.

After coming second in the European Championships, I returned to Colorado for the 1975 World Championships, and lo and behold, there was life in the old dog yet! I came third and astounded everybody. When I arrived initially, everybody had smirked and said: 'Oh God, he's come back for some more punishment!' But I really skated quite well, and the tune changed.

The months that followed continued this vein, with Mr Fassi and everything else being splendid. The happiest winter of my life was that leading up to the Olympics. We were all staying at the same hotel, in Garmisch, and although the temperatures were freezing there, somehow I was able to cope with it in a way that I had not been able to before. Mr Fassi was very human about the whole thing and if I got too cold he would send me off the ice to get warm. He would rather have had me skate well for twenty minutes when it was warm, than for three hours

with a friend in Colorado

when it was sub-zero. As a result we laughed and it was *fun*, even though we worked very hard. Also, everything was very well taken care of; the organisation never flagged. My nervousness, too, was less of a problem. After Munich, I had been so concerned about my inability to control my nerves that at the following World Championships I managed to hold on by pure consciousness and will-power, even though I was shaking like a leaf in a hurricane. Something had to be done.

A number of my friends had spoken in the past of Erhard Seminar Training, a form of therapy much in use in America. I went to a Guest Seminar, and I must admit that I disliked the people, the atmosphere, and everything about it, but there are rare moments in my life when a course of action seems not only right but inevitable – almost preordained – and in one of those moments I decided to take the course. I telephoned Mr Fassi and told him that I would be staying in New York for an extra two weeks as there was something that I wanted to do. Mr Fassi was worried that I would miss vital training, but I was adamant and he realised there was nothing he could do. 'Oh, all right,' he said mournfully.

When I got back, he was astounded by a number of things. In the two-week period that I was away I had made up my Olympic 'programme' – in twenty minutes. In fifteen minutes I had the music all edited. The result, the *Don Quixote* programme, may seem to be a very basic one, but it was effective and it worked. And I loved doing it. After having concocted it in that first twenty minutes I went through it again the following day and nothing had altered. From that moment on I could always do it; it was very strange – as if someone had waved a magic wand over me. When I got back to Colorado, where I was not noted for my stamina (Denver being at a very high altitude) I immediately asked Mr Fassi to watch my new programme, being anxious to know what he thought of it. 'Oh, you can't do it today; you'll kill yourself,' said Mr Fassi. But I said: 'Well, just watch it anyway,' and I put the record on and I did the programme – without any mistakes. Mr Fassi looked at me, rather bemused. 'Mmm – it's quite good.' And Mrs Fassi said: 'Oooh – it's *very* nice. I *like* that!'

The following day, Mr Fassi said: 'If you feel well enough, I'd like you to try a few parts of the programme.' I did the whole thing without stopping, and there it was again. 'Oh, that's quite good; that's got a lot of possibilities. That's not bad!' Although Mr Fassi warned me that I had better not do the programme the following day as I would be too tired, I had decided by then that I was not going to stop any more. I was not going to be tired any more. I *was* tired, but I did not stop. And it worked; everything worked.

Gradually, it all became like a game. Every evening at six o'clock I would do the *Don Quixote* programme and eventually we had reached something like twenty-five run-throughs without my making a mistake. I was always 'on', never missing a jump, or two-footing, or missing a beat. The whole thing became something of a lark. When we arrived in Europe and began practices, I never considered that it would be anything other than right. In the past, if I had gone to a competition where I was feeling tired, I would not do the whole programme at the run-through for fear of people thinking that I was out of condition. I would endeavour to do small, bright parts here and there. Now, with my new programme, it was all different. Suddenly, I appeared as a very consistent person who could churn out a programme mechanically, and the sight began to undermine the confidence of the other competitors.

But Mr Fassi never believed that EST had anything to do with the change. One day, in the cloak-rooms, I was being interviewed by a reporter, and EST was mentioned. The reporter turned to Mr Fassi and asked him what *he* thought about it. 'Well,' said Mr Fassi, 'everybody has got to believe in something, so I let him believe in that!' He really thought that I was playing some strange confidence trick on myself. But recently he has asked me for the address, so perhaps he feels that my extra two weeks in New York can be forgiven.

final win in the British National Championships, 1975

Prior to the vital season containing the Olympics, the British Championships were scheduled for early December 1975, which from an Olympic-training point of view was early; I knew it would be unwise to be at peak form so soon. However, I did travel to England from Denver and I thought that my form, though not good at that stage, would be

Back in Denver, I worked solidly for another month before we travelled back for the European Championships in Geneva. This was to be the occasion of Jan Hoffman's return to skating after two years' absence with leg injuries; so we were to have a former World Champion in the field; we had Kovalev, reigning European Champion; and we had Volkov, reigning World Champion. We were set for a competition containing three European Champions and two World Champions, all competing against one another as a foretaste of the Olympics.

skating the 'Rachmaninov' short-programme

enough to win. As it transpired, that view was correct, but in the long free-skating programme I took a very bad fall while making the first jump. I recovered sufficiently to win the over-all title by a clear margin, but onlookers and officials were rather shaken by the whole thing, and their concern was evident. They could not really know that I had never attempted to give the performance of my life at that stage; had I planned to do so, then by January and February I would have been over the top.

far left, top:
a forward Ena Bauer; that is a wide 4th position, travelling sideways

far left, bottom:
a gliding pose camouflaging the preparation for a triple jump, and in the process collecting mental and physical composure

SEPP SCHÖNMETZLER

MICK DESABZENS

above:
backwards landing of a double lutz jump, the right arm being raised high not only to add line, but also to remind one not to 'collapse' in the rib cage

left:
another camouflaged preparation, this time in a forward attitude

European Championships

In the initial stages of the competition I came second in the school figures. I thought, myself, that the figures I did then were the best I had ever done at a European Championship. Then came the compulsory short programme, in which my piece set to Rachmaninov was on display in Europe for the first time. The actual ruling of the short programme demands six prescribed elements to be skated to a piece of music of no longer than two minutes' duration. One is supposed to do the six elements and the judges give two sets of marks – one lot for the technical precision of the elements themselves, and another set for the manner of presentation. While one is awarded marks for artistic impression, almost any movement other than the six prescribed can be interpreted as further elements, if one wants to be totally pedantic. It was an aspect of the competitions that always confused me.

However, in the practice sessions I duly began to perform my new short programme, and at the point where I was to execute a double axel I thought: 'This is really too plain and boring for words.' So I decided to precede the double axel with a big spread-eagle, from which I would launch myself straight into the jump. It seemed to me to be effective and it helped the programme by being placed dramatically. Too dramatically, as events proved, because Mr Fassi came to me two days before the competition with disturbing news.

He had heard, in a very 'round the corner' way, that the Russian judges had been going to all the other judges (with the obvious exception of the British judge) and they had been pointing out that I was doing a programme with an 'illegal' element in it. 'Even if he does everything *perfectly*, you will still be able to penalise him for using an illegal element!' Our informant was in fact a Russian teacher who felt that the whole campaign was so unfair that he was determined to try and prevent it. Carlo Fassi's plan was very simple. 'Keep practising the programme exactly as you have been doing it. Change nothing. But in the competition itself, don't do it; don't do the spread-eagle! Just skate backwards and go straight into a double axel.'

And I did. Panic registered on numerous judges' faces. Where was the illegal element? I doubt that they had paid much attention to the programme itself, so anxious were they to register the crime. I had skated quite well, the judges were flummoxed, and there was a general uproar. The Russian contingent was plainly amazed and mystified. Then the marks came up and a great wall of average marks left me in second position. It was at that point that I said to myself: 'I am *never* going to win anything.' There I was, doing my utmost, the competition against me was nothing spectacular on the day, and yet I seemed unable to make any impression on the majority of the judges. But I went on with the free programme, performing it in a very determined, very 'tight' manner and I made no mistakes; nothing that could be labelled as such by the judges.

At the time I came off the ice I still did not know that I had won. There was a long delay and a great clamour going on, and I really felt very depressed. Again I had skated very early in the programme, and the marks had not seemed particularly good even though I had skated well. We sat around for about half an hour before discovering that the seemingly impossible had happened – I had won. Carlo came bounding around, shouting: 'Ya got it! Ya got it! We did it! We beat them all in one time!' There had always been a joke around that if it was not one Russian at the top it was certainly going to be another. Even more surprising, I won because of one judge from the Eastern bloc, a Czechoslovakian. His marking was decisive; it was the first time that an Eastern European judge had voted for a Western skater. It was all that we needed, and a very dramatic turning point. What was even more extraordinary was the fact that I had been totally unaware of that particular judge. Usually, when one does the figures, one notices the nine judges standing by, and one gets to know exactly who they all are, but of this particular man I had no recollection whatsoever. It was only later during an exhibition tour, when we were in Brnö, that a man came up to me in the street and said, with the aid of an interpreter: 'I am the judge from Czechoslovakia who put you first!' To which I replied, rather lamely: 'Well, thank you very much!' 'No – not thank you,' he replied. 'I got into trouble, but what I did was right.' For less than a minute I spoke to that man, and I never saw him again, but he it was who made the vital difference to everything that followed. Ironically, a Russian, and then a Czech, paved the way for my Olympic medal. Had it not been for them, I would have arrived at the Olympic Games as a Silver Medallist and I am convinced in my own mind that such a tag would have carried less weight than the fact that I had beaten them all in Geneva, where the Eastern judges were thick on the ground.

It is true that for years there had been uproars from the crowds concerning my marks in competitions, but the judges always ruled the day. In 1976 I 'packaged' my presentation in a very deliberate manner; I made sure that I gave them everything that they wanted to see. I must be honest and admit that I set out to win, I did not do the programmes as I had done them in previous years, with all the elements that meant most to me; this time I actually wanted to *win*, and I knew that if I did certain things, then I could win. If my programmes still seemed 'artistic' to the judges, they could not say that they were lacking in any technicalities required by them. Before, I had 'camouflaged' those difficult

technicalities because that is the way in which I like to present myself on the ice; I hate telegraphed movements. But in 1976 I set out to make the difficulties plainly apparent. And it worked. Suddenly there were people coming up to me, saying: 'But I had no *idea* you could do all those jumps! When did you learn to do all those things?' Of course, I had been doing them all the time, but now I had packaged them in an obvious manner, with simple music, basic manner, basic steps; and suddenly it *looked* difficult. By aiming 'low' I had achieved a 'high' from a judging point of view.

The night of my European victory, there were lots of high spirits; it was really very exciting to win that competition. It was in the exhibition programme, after the competition, that I fell over. I had a rule that I never did triple jumps in exhibitions; to me a double turn in the air looks just as nice as a triple; in fact it usually looks better because one gets more 'air' in the jump and one does not scrunch so much. But because the Olympics were coming up, Mr Fassi told me to do a triple loop, and although I normally did a double in that particular piece, on this occasion I put in a triple – and of course fell over! It made great television action-replay material for weeks to come. Every time anyone mentioned my name, there would be the action-replay of me hitting the deck in Geneva!

eft: final pose of the Don Quixote' programme

below: a half-loop jump in the Geneva exhibition programme

E.J PRESS

DIMITRI SOULAS

Going to the Olympics had always been a great goal for me, from the time when I was quite young. Eventually, in 1968, I found myself listed for Grenoble as Reserve, but the longed-for position in the team itself did not materialise. Four years later I was actually in the team for the Olympics at Sapporo; I had made it, even if I was buried in the middle as one of the also-rans. The Japanese did wonderful things for the Opening Ceremony, not least with the weather, which had been awful right up until the moment of the opening, when the clouds seemed suddenly to roll themselves neatly into paper-bags and vanish for several hours. There were helicopters showering pink roses into the air, along with thousands of doves and balloons swirling above the beautiful stadium.

In the stadium everybody sported their 'regalia', the Olympics being something of a fashion show, along with all else. I stood there in the midst of our team, overpowered by the realisation that my lifetime's ambition had been fulfilled. But around me were people to whom the Olympics meant nothing more than the price of a bob-sleigh holiday in Switzerland – an incredible group of blasé dilettantes who were there with no thought of earnest competition and who made the Opening Ceremony an occasion for ribald and facetious jokes. If they were aiming to bring the whole thing down to their own level, then they certainly succeeded. I always felt that the Olympic Games was an event which, as an ideal, was there for one to take or leave as one saw fit; but I knew that once there, under the umbrella of the organisation, one had a moral obligation to respect it. For me, the excitement surrounding the lighting of the Olympic flame is indescribable. At Sapporo I longed for someone to be standing near me who would share the same feelings, but those around me seemed to find yet another excuse for a snigger or a slice of cheap sarcasm.

top left, opposite: advice from Mrs Fassi, while Mr Fassi watches another pupil

below: with Dorothy Hamill – two Olympic hopefuls from the Fassi stable

1976 Olympic Games

Four years later I found myself in the British team again, this time for the Games at Innsbruck. There had been a tremendous burst of publicity after my win at the European Championships of 1976; suddenly there was the scent of a medal. Everyone was anxious to take good care of me. I had been training in Garmisch with Mr Fassi and I arrived after the rest of the team, but there was no demur. Everything was rather 'special': a quiet room for once and lots of minor attentions. I got on with my training and then the great Opening Ceremony came around once again.

This time, I was told that I was to be the flag-bearer and that I was to march twelve feet ahead of the rest of the team. Standing in close file waiting to enter the arena, I heard the same crass remarks and the same brand of cynicism that had scarred the Ceremony four years earlier. Nothing seemed to have altered. But this time I had a wonderful twelve-foot 'cushion' between my idealism and the ribaldry behind me. And I had the flag. That, for me, represented my own efforts in attaining a position where I could actually enjoy (albeit on my own) that which I had set out to enjoy. It was a very happy moment and I was genuinely proud to do it; I took everything very seriously and wanted to do it all with as much panache as I could muster. It seemed important to me then, and it still seems important to me. As we stepped into the arena I was suddenly out of earshot, and I no longer cared about the belittling; for better or worse I was in a nationalistic vacuum of my own devising.

I should be honest and say that of all the competitions I had ever been in, from the first Hop, Skip and Jump event when I was seven, I had never been more sure of winning anything than I was of winning that Gold Medal. This will be treated as an extraordinary remark, but I had so programmed myself that I was going to win that I went through the whole thing in a very calm and collected manner.

"School figures" skated at the Olympic Games

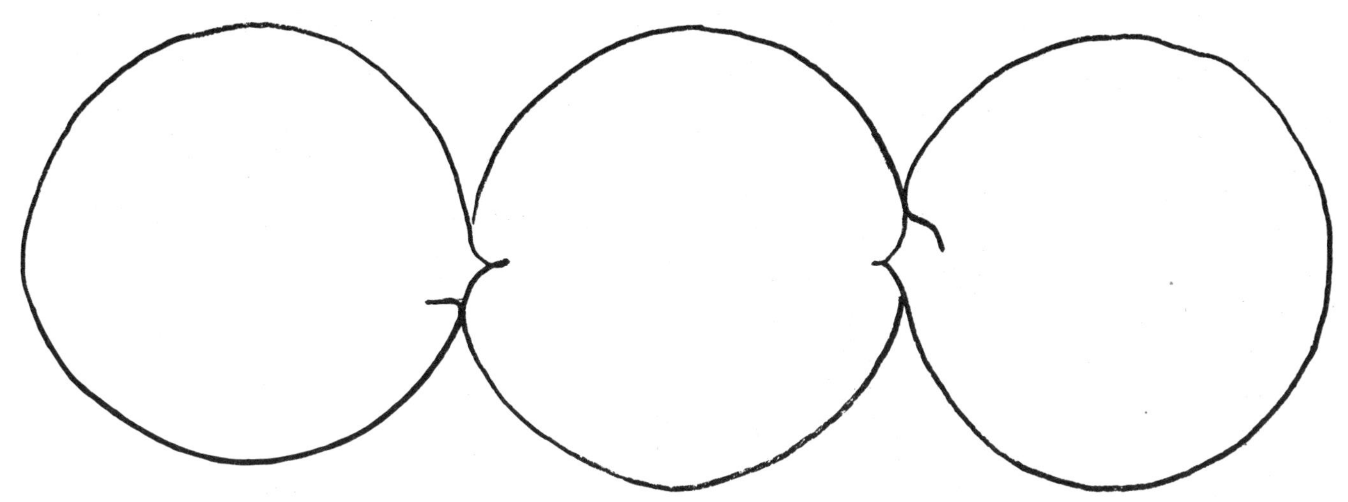

RIGHT OUTSIDE ROCKER.

A.P. WIRE

Skating a right forward outside rocker, during the school figures section of the Olympic Games. Dr Suzanne Francis, the Canadian judge, was subsequently suspended for one year by the Technical Figures Committee of the International Skating Union

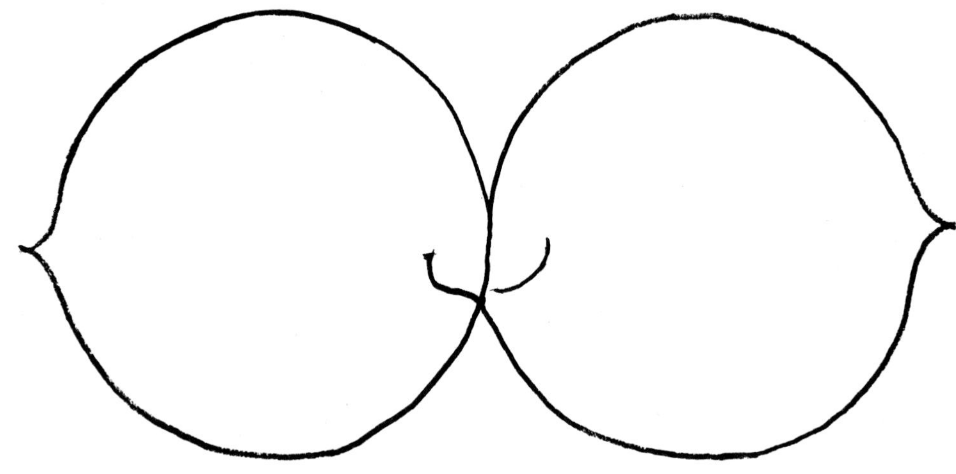

LEFT BACKWARDS PARAGRAPH BRACKET.

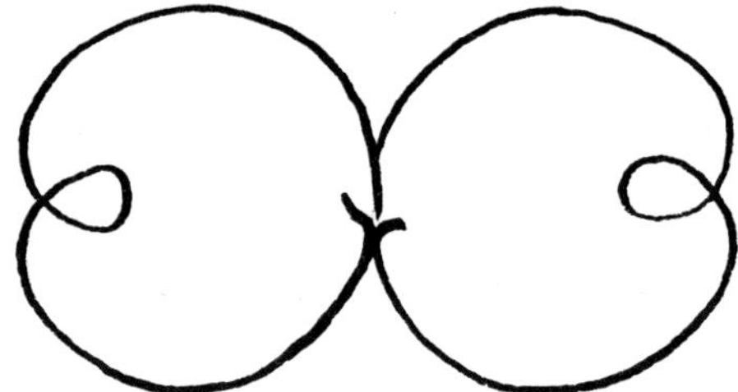

RIGHT FORWARD PARAGRAPH LOOP.

After the compulsory figures I was in second position, which was perfect for me, because although first place might have been even more agreeable at that stage, the skater who was ahead of me was one of the weakest free-skaters in the competition. He had not gained a top place at the European Championships. After my good figures, the short free-programme came next, in which I did my two-minute Rachmaninov piece – never one of my favourite programmes, but still I won it and this placed me very squarely in the lead. At the same time, the boy who had been first in the figures now dropped to second, putting a nice 'padding' between me and the others. And my strongest part of the competition was coming up. I could conceive that a couple of the boys might have beaten me in the short programme, but my actual win at that stage removed most of the pressure.

Then there was a day free, which was terrible; everything seemed to take an eternity. I had all but done the whole thing and there seemed no way to fill in the time until the actual completion. The free-skating was not due until the following evening, so there was much of the following day to fill as well. At least in the Olympic Village there is that marvellous sense of protection; no distracting outside agencies can penetrate. Although I was excited I was also confident, and I suspect that I radiated this to the other competitors. There had been a bad influenza scare and people kept coming up to me and asking if I was all right. 'Of *course* I'm all right,' I replied, '*I'm* not going to be ill!' I went for a long walk in the morning, and I said something to Glyn Watts to the effect of 'If I win tonight. . . .' I got a marvellously stinging reply: 'Don't you start 'iffing' at me. This is the first time I've heard you say "If" all winter. Now say the whole thing again, only with the word "after" at the beginning of the sentence.' So I said the words 'After I win . . . .' This sounds

below: the short free-programme, skated to Rachmaninov's last variation on a theme by Paganini

conceited and unpleasant; everything that reflects the thrusting side of competition, but that was not the real basis of the psychology.

For the free-skating draw I emerged as first skater for the second half of the competition, which is the worst place to skate. My fellow competitors were delighted with that position falling to me, but Mr Fassi said in a rather loud voice: 'That is *wonderful*! He gives so much pressure to the others.' And with that we left. We did not even bother to wait and see where the others were skating. 'Hexellent. Great! They will be so nervous after you skate,' continued Mr Fassi for all within earshot. He had worked out my schedule to the last detail: which bus to catch, when to arrive at the rink, when to put my skates on. And I was fine. I was not nervous in the slightest degree; it was extraordinary. I also did what I had learned to do that winter: I went to my room (private this time) and I went into my 'space'; I shut my eyes and took a 'step' outside my body and examined my body in very close detail, and found out that it was in very good working order. Mentally I 'played a film' of myself doing my programme (without mistakes in it) and after that I simply opened my eyes and proceeded to the warm-up. That too was fine. My warm-ups have always been the same; almost choreographed. I used to skate around twice, do a waltz jump, an axel, do a double loop, a double salchow, a double toe-loop, a double axel and then another double toe-loop, and then go and stand by the side and wait. Mr Fassi had prepared me to skate in every possible position of the draw. For instance, on a Monday I would do a warm-up for six minutes, as if I was skating first. On Tuesday I would do a six minute warm-up and then have to have six minutes off, as if I was skating second. On Wednesday I would do it as if I was skating in the third position; and so on for the remainder of the week, at the end of which I had experienced every variation in time-scale. I did actually like skating first as one does not have to go off after the warm-up; one stays on the ice and has the feel of it. It so happened that the ice was too hard that day. There had been a hockey match that afternoon and the temperature of the ice had not been properly restored. Because of this I made a mental note to over-compensate by bending my knees a bit more. Back to Mr Vickers' very first advice!

I went out on the signal, skated to my starting place, and then said to myself: 'The next five minutes are going to determine the rest of your life. So have them go the way you want them to.' There have been very few occasions in my life when I have skated and it did *all* 'come together'. Then it did; it came together technically, physically and mentally, and it all came together so easily and so naturally that it was absolutely no effort. I was not even out of breath at the end. I was aware, at a subconscious level, of the crowd being 'for' me, but the only outside thoughts that went through my mind were to do with the cameras. There were hundreds of them, and every time that I hit any sort of shape that was remotely approaching a correct position or something that would make a 'shot', there would be a long, drawn-out barrage of camera clatter, almost like computer chatter. It was deafening. It almost distracted me; in fact it did distract me to the extent that I was conscious of it. I was always fairly sure of landing those three triples, and after landing the third of them I was almost equally sure of landing everything else and of being able to do the rest of the programme without a mistake. As I landed that last one, I thought: 'You've just won the Olympics, kid, so enjoy the rest of it!' And I did; it was completely enjoyable.

At the end, all sorts of flowers cascaded onto the ice, but for once in my life I did not pick them up myself. Suddenly there were other people doing that. And I let them do it; I do not know why. Normally I always went and picked up at least one, but this time I took a bow, went off, and waited. I simply was not thinking about those kind tributes; it was only when I saw the films later that I realised that I had not picked up any of the flowers. I was pleased, and I thought: 'Okay; you've done it,' but I was not in any state of euphoria. It was still the old Vickers style: 'Go out and do it and come straight off. Don't hang around.' The Fassis were obviously very pleased but we did not jump up and down or anything; we were all remarkably calm.

Beyond the curtains, where the television viewer never sees, it was like walking from tranquillity into bedlam. The furore was extraordinary, and it must have been awful for the other competitors who had still to skate; there were seven competitors still to go, but it was physically impossible for anyone else to win at that stage, because of my marks. Having extricated myself from the cameras and the interviewers, I went to my room, while Mr Fassi said: 'I go watch the others.' The team leader, Eileen Anderson, came in as I was taking my boots off, and she kissed me, and was crying. I think that at that point perhaps I shed a tear as well. It was at that precise moment that a journalist handed me a Press article in manuscript form, and because I did not stop and read the entire thing through then and there, the newspapers were full of articles the following day based on that wire service 'interview', which laid bare thoughts and comments garnered from me in previous days and which had no relevance and bearing whatsoever to the winning of a Gold Medal. With the medal, it seemed that I had acquired all the trappings that went with it; the chains as well as the ribbons. Well, so be it – but it is a foreign jungle to me.

GEORGE KONIG

an inside spread-eagle during the Olympic free-skating programme

GEORGE KONIG

with Vladimir Kovalev and Toller Cranston, silver and bronze medallists

After all the conflicting emotions surrounding the Olympic win, the morning afterwards I went out to Seefeld, beyond Innsbruck, with my mother and brother and a lot of my mother's friends who had come out with her to the Games. This was a day of calm before a terrible and rather frightening Press conference back in Innsbruck, the direct result of the extraordinary Press release of the day before. However, it passed off satisfactorily.

The next morning I had arranged to meet Mr Fassi and Mr Mosler for breakfast. This was something of a prearranged plan, because Carlo had said to me, way back in November: 'It doesn't matter whether you win the European or not, but you must win the Olympics, and when you've done that you must *finish*. You musn't go to the World Championships.' I had said: 'Why not?' He was thinking for my own good when he replied: 'If you win the Olympics it is worth so much more than the World title, even in cash terms. When you win, everyone looks at you twice as hard and they try to find a way to 'un-win' you. We are not going to let anybody do that! After you win, you quit, and you go home, and that's it! Don't tell anybody this – we just go home, and we don't go for the World!' (It turned out that he had said exactly the same thing to Dorothy Hamill, and we had both, in the end, agreed to this plan.) With an Olympic Gold Medal in our hands we were sitting around at nine in the morning, eating eggs and bacon, like three of the glummest people in the world. Mr Mosler added that he thought going to the World Championships was a big risk, but in the final analysis I ought to do what I wanted. 'So what if you win World Championships,' went on Carlo, 'it means nothing! No one watches. The television, they don't care; nothing.'

DAILY MAIL

So, rather reluctantly, I agreed to the plan. I left the hotel thinking: 'Well – that's it. Your competitive days are over. You'll never have to worry about school figures ever again. No more triple-toe-loop combinations or anything like that, ever again!' Far from feeling that a burden had been taken from my shoulders, I felt a total depression. But I kept quiet about 'the plan'. I was blandly non-committal whenever the subject of Sweden and the World Championships arose.

At the Closing Ceremony for the Games, there was an exhibition on the rink by all the medallists. By this time there was so much publicity surrounding me; so much analysis of my skating, of my character – even down to my toothbrush it seemed – that it was the one time in my life when I went out onto the ice totally inhibited by everything that I had heard and read about myself in those few mad days. Everything that had, in the past, seemed a normal course of events now seemed to carry some hidden significance. From my early days I had always worn stage make-up on the ice for the simple reason that I go quite green in the face and the sight is far from pleasant for onlookers. Now, I thought: 'No – I can't wear make-up. For the first time someone will notice.' As I was running through my programme in my mind, I kept thinking: 'No – I musn't do that – someone will think it is effeminate. No – I had better not do that either. . . .' Suddenly it seemed that I could not do anything that I had been doing for years.

And then I found myself out on the ice and I thought: 'To hell with it! I'm going to do everything just the way I want to.' And I did, and a lot of people thought that was the best I had ever skated. I really quite enjoyed doing it; it was my *Scheherazade* piece. Some people said afterwards: 'I've never seen you skate with so much aggression and determination; it was as if you you were really fighting out there!' Normally, I never look as if I am struggling when I am skating, but on this occasion it showed. I suppose I was fighting a lot of things. Even Mr Fassi thought it was the best he had seen, and so did Mrs Fassi. After that, the flags came down and everybody packed up and went home.

SEQUENCE MICK DESARZENS

exhibition performance, to 'Scheherazade', at the Olympic Games Closing Ceremony

I spent a week back in England, and it was like being in an insane asylum. I had never quite realised the full extent of the coverage and the publicity concerning the Gold Medal; the whole furore took me completely unawares. I almost panicked; I could not understand how, wherever I went, people recognised me. I came into London with Penny Malec, and it was extraordinary. People ran out of shops; cars would stop right in the middle of the traffic while the drivers got out; taxi drivers held up the traffic to let me cross the street; it was really most odd, and rather bewildering. Almost everyone in the street was doing 'double-takes', like in an old movie. I suppose my curly hair might have helped the recognition process, though it was far from unusual with young people. I had mine curled at that time for a particular reason. I am prone to thinness, especially when I am working hard, and the previous summer I had been ill with an internal parasite from one of the 'hot' countries. As a result of this I was looking like the proverbial rake. The sight of my own skull in the mirror depressed me. Even my hair had lost its usual slight wave, so I thought curly hair might make me look cheerful and healthy, even though I was neither. Thus the curly hair came back to England, along with the medal.

World Championships 1976

At that time I was invited to be a Guest of Honour at the Guildhall, where they were making awards for Valour in Sport. It was the first time that I had been in the Guildhall and the whole luncheon seemed a marvellous occasion, even though I had been persuaded to make a speech, which was televised. Naturally, I spoke about the lack of facilities and the lack of finance for British sportsmen. People, just at that moment, were ready to listen to almost anything that I might utter, so it was a good moment to try and make certain important points about the lack of aid for sports in our country. After my own effort I was sitting there listening to all sorts of wonderful people and hearing what they had done, and I felt totally out of place; I felt I had not done anything at all that remotely suggested courage or valour.

It was at that moment that I suddenly made up my mind about the World Championships. I did not care in the least whether I won or lost, I simply knew that I was going. I think the whole occasion in the Guildhall had left me rather moved, and I thought how disappointing it would be for anyone who had any form of enthusiasm for my performances in the European Championships and the Olympics to think that I could not in some way face the final challenge in sporting terms. I suppose I had many reasons for wanting to go: my pride; to prove that it was not all luck; and perhaps most important, I wanted to prove to myself that I could face again the possibility of *not* winning.

I went back to Richmond where I was staying, and I got on the telephone to Helsinki where Mr Fassi was working with the others. He said: 'You're crazy; don't be a fool! You've had a week off; you can't do it!' But I was determined, and above all I really did not care if I did not win. Mr Fassi said: '*Please* don't come.' 'I'm coming tomorrow at ten o'clock,' I said. 'I ask you one more time – *please don't come*!' pleaded Mr Fassi on the line. I told him I *was* going, and he said, finally: 'All right. But just remember: it was your decision.'

In Helsinki we had the worst week imaginable. Mr Fassi was nervous, convinced that I was going to get pulverised in the competition. I was so out of form it was almost unbelievable; there was nothing I could do, not even if my life had depended on it. For once my long-standing discipline totally disappeared. I never completed a practice programme. I would fall over, or miss twenty things in the first thirty seconds. Mr Fassi stood on the sidelines, watching this débâcle and pleading with me to go home again. But I would not, and finally we set off for the World Championships at Gothenburg.

It was a very hard competition for me in many ways; not necessarily

left: congratulations from Mrs Ulrich Salchow (as in triple!) and her daughter

to do with the performance. I was happy just to be there, but the Press was having a field day. I was public property and it seemed that I could be taken apart and displayed in any manner they chose. The Swedish Press stopped at nothing from the moment I descended the steps of the aircraft. Mr Fassi and I were actually 'bugged'; we discovered microphones pushed along the barriers where we were working. Faced with all this I refused to talk, so the journalists' life ambition became one of getting me to do so.

Somehow we ploughed on through all the harassment to the point of the competition itself. On the day of the school figures, when we were training on the ice, Mr Fassi had said to me: 'John! Just look at the ice. Look at what you are doing!' I had done one figure very badly. He said: 'What can I tell you? What can I say to shock you into realising what you are doing?' Of course I knew, and there was nothing he could say. I went out and did that particular figure, which was a bracket, and I came fourth or fifth, and when I saw the

PRESSENS BILD AB

marks they *did* shock me! 'Why don't you withdraw?' said Mr Fassi at this point. But there was a loop to do next, and I assured him that I would be good. 'Well that's what you said *last* time!' came the retort. But I did a good loop and I won that figure. I think that was the best loop I ever did. Mr Fassi was marginally more pacified. So we both hung on in there. I ended in second position, and not such a good second as I had been at the corresponding stage of the Olympics. Mrs Fassi had the unpleasant task of taking me for my practice for the short free programme. This was at seven in the morning – *not* my best time! Ever since the Olympics I had not been able to do the triple combination. 'Now come on,' said Mrs Fassi. 'Just warm up and then try it very quietly. You know you can do it; we've done it a million times.' But I fell, ceaselessly. In the end I said to her: 'Look, you know as well as I do that I can't do it this morning, but I'll do it this afternoon!' In fact I did, really well. It was the one time when my mind went completely blank though, and at the end I put my foot down – for no possible reason – which discounted the jump. I was 'away'; goodness knows where. As luck would have it, the boy who was in the lead made a worse mess in the short programme, so by a rather freak chance I stayed in second place, and the boy who did skate best in the short programme was so far behind that he had no chance of catching up, whatever he did. I had made a mistake; I was still second; suddenly the pressure was off again. Although, at that point, it looked as if Kovalev would win, I knew that my long free-skating programme was better than his and I knew also that his temperament was suspect at vital moments.

As I left the hotel that evening to go to the rink, another front-page picture of myself stared out from the news-stand in the foyer. In the picture I looked distraught, and Carlo had been caught as well, looking anguished. There seemed to be acres of Swedish text connected with it, like a thousand consonants shunted together, and my curiosity for once got the better of me. I said to the lady on the reception desk: 'What does that say?' She did not really want to tell me but I insisted, and she translated the heading which said something to the effect that 'The Great Olympic Champion Cannot Make Any Mistakes Tonight', going on to point out that Sweden would in all probability see my downfall within a few hours. And I thought: 'Well – that's very true; that really *is* true.'

I went out onto the ice knowing that I really could not afford a single error, and I did not make one and I think, looking back on it, that it was probably the best competition programme that I have ever done. I was determined; I told myself that I was not going to make a mistake, or fall over;

Left: landing a triple toe-loop with grim determination, during the free-skating programme

even if I came second they were going to have to say that it was a good performance, that I had not fluffed it. There had also been a succession of people coming up to me, saying: 'You've skated *so* well in the last two major competitions; you can't possibly do it a third time!' And I would think: 'That's ridiculous. Of *course* I can.' I was really very relieved when it was finally over. I had won. I think it is true to say that my composure did at last crack a little when I received my medal, because I knew I had finished, I knew I had finished as well as anyone could have finished, and I knew that, in some way, I had proved some point that I had been trying to make, however subconsciously. Mr Mosler had prearranged a dinner for me, for after the competition. I cannot imagine what it would have been had I not won; a wake I suppose, or perhaps it would have been conveniently forgotten. However, there was a room set aside in the hotel and I was the last to arrive, having had to change and go through the usual dope-test and formalities that go with such competitions, including the ever-present Press corps. By the time one gets to any dinner in such circumstances everyone else has finished eating, and this was no exception; I walked in to the partial wreckage of the meal and took my seat. Nobody said a word, and then Mr Mosler cleared his throat and said: 'Well – you're a damned fool! But I'm glad you did it.' And that was all. They were all correct in thinking, before, that I had 'gone', and of course I had. I *was* over the top.

above: the medal ceremony at the 1976 World Championships, with Vladimir Kovalev and Jan Hoffman

left: as the television viewers saw it

right: with Carlo and Christa Fassi; three very relieved people

BILD SERVICE

with Dorothy Hamill after the World Championships exhibition programme – which included a sailor's hornpipe

After the World Championships my one ambition was to go back to New York; I begged to be excused the World Tour that is usually obligatory after the big competitions. I just wanted to curl up in a ball somewhere, so I pleaded with Mr Fassi, but he said: 'Look, it's the last time. Go off and have fun. Do eighteen exhibitions in twenty days!' I agreed finally to go as far as the halfway mark, which was London. It was obvious I had to go as far as London. I had been going off on those tours since I was seventeen and they have never been easy. One goes into a town, warms up, does the show and then departs immediately – to begin all over again the following day, somewhere else. Lo and behold, on this final tour I had the best time I could remember. I did my Olympic programme every night, plop, plop, plop; all fun and no problems. I did have the agreement with the International Skating Union about my being able to leave the tour after London, but as several other people had also made the same decision, the team was going to look terribly understrength. After an all-night party in Richmond, with no sleep at all, I packed up my things and set off again – to Czechoslovakia! A journey that should have taken six hours took us thirty-six hours, on a train caught in snow.

We went all through Eastern Europe, those of us that remained. As a result, I did my very last amateur performance in Moscow, and I thought this was really rather appropriate. Again, I found myself *determined* – I was going to go in there and show them! I was there, and I was still kicking and they were going to have to look at me. All the rows of stony faces in the Official Box were trapped in their seats while I was out there on the ice. It was a moment to relish. The actual Russian people themselves *do* enjoy my skating, strangely enough. I even did an extra encore, which is something I very seldom do. But it was Russia, I was happy, it was all but over, and those people who had tried to stop me for all those years were having to go on watching. Midnight in Moscow: that was the end of my amateur career. It was over at last.

top: during the BBC TV Scene programme for children, which included elementary instruction before the cameras

left: voted by poll BBC TV Sports Personality of the Year, 1976

BBC

BBC

BBC

Christmas Day Television Special 1976

For London Weekend Television, I wanted to skate to a very Hot Jazz, Blues-ey piece, and they found *I got it Bad, and that ain't Good.* Norman Maen wanted the item on the smallest possible area. It turned out to be one of those cases where one's original concept and what actually emerges are very far removed from one another. I had wanted it to be 'hot and sweaty' in style, with earthy, casual clothes. It came out looking like *Vogue*. The number gave me great problems. I could not understand why Norman wanted me to skate on a piece of ice about twelve feet by fifteen; I could not grasp his concept. But I think he was right and it was an interesting exercise in confinement, though not what I had envisaged initially.

LONDON WEEKEND TV

skating with Peggy Fleming in 'Send in the Clowns'

In the television show I had chosen the pieces that I wanted to do, and they had included *Afternoon of a Faun*. The producer, John Scoffield, added one piece, *Polovtsian Dances*, in which I bounded around among a lot of terrified musicians perched on the ice. I was against doing my Olympic programme again, but they wanted it done and I could understand why, so that went in as well. My partner in *Faun* was Peggy Fleming. I had skated with Peggy during June of that year, in a Gala at Denver, and when I worked with her in California I had choreographed *Send in the Clowns* for us to perform together in a Gala, rather than doing our usual solo performances. She really is the easiest person to skate with, and I asked her if she could appear with me in the television show, but by the time she arrived in England she was pregnant, and so I was scared that I would bump her, or drop her, or knock her over, or even just tire her. Women are very brave about being pregnant; to them it is the most normal thing in the world, and they know how strong they are. She was in England for about three weeks and I watched her change visibly during that time, and I got more scared as every day passed. It turned out to be a boy. Actually, I *knew* that it would be!

LONDON WEEKEND TV

from Aldeburgh
to
New York

Outdoor Skating

Perhaps because of my childhood fears, I still do not like skating on natural ice, and I do not like performing outdoors either, because of the added difficulties. But skating for pleasure on an outdoor rink is highly enjoyable; every breath of wind blows one around and alters one's balance, which is fun to contend with when no competition is at stake. At the Rockefeller Plaza, the outdoor winter rink is well below street level, so that there is very little wind, and the spectators on Fifth Avenue have a natural balcony-view down onto the ice. It is wonderful to be down there on the ice and looking up at the great skyscrapers against the sky; when I do a spin they whirl around. In New York, the Wollman Rink in Central Park is also very enjoyable.

Normally I am too shy to skate on a public rink during the daytime; it is no fun to me *just* to skate around; I always like to skate freely and properly. But late at night I sometimes go to the Rockefeller rink around eleven o'clock, just before it closes, when there are only one or two people about. In the Spring the air is warm and the stars are often out and the whole place seems very beautiful, and skating for pleasure is then a real delight. I have been in several Benefit performances at the Rockefeller Center, particularly for the United Hospital Fund, an American medical aid foundation.

I have also done Benefit performances at Madison Square Garden, one of those 'special' buildings with an atmosphere and magic all of its own. One thinks of all the great events that have taken place there and it becomes, somehow, rather inspiring. Because it is so huge, it is actually a difficult building to skate in; everything looks the same from every angle. The East and West sides of the auditorium look identical, and the North and South sides likewise, so it becomes hard to know exactly where one is during a performance. Normally, during a spin, one can catch sight of odd things that register a direction and bring one 'home' again, but at Madison Square Garden there is nothing to latch on to, to give one a bearing. Also, because it is so enormous, one gets the feeling that, to most of the spectators, one must look the size of an ant. But I have been lucky there; because I find the atmosphere so stimulating, I have usually skated well at the place, even when running a very high temperature – as I had on my first appearance. One gets through because of that atmosphere.

JAN V.A

Russian split jump

Butterfly jump

TONY DUFFY

Stag jump

These three pictures sum up everything that I, personally, do not want to see much of in skating. I think some movements are spectacularly difficult physical feats, but I happen to think that they are also extremely ugly; Butterflies and Russian Split Jumps, for example. Split Jumps look fine on the floor, where one can point one's feet, but they look horrible on the ice, where there is no way that one can hide the fact that the feet cannot be turned out – they would have to be facing backwards!

As a result, I have never really done these 'dashing' skating movements except for the benefit of photographers in earlier years, when these particular pictures were taken. Sports photographers always want one to be upside down in the air with one's feet above one's head. All those things are really the easiest things in the world to do, as far as I am concerned. By the time I had stopped giving in to requests for these explosive positions for cameras, and had reverted to poses with good line, I was always asked 'Can't you do anything spectacular?' And I always replied: 'No – I can't do anything spectacular!'

The Stag Jump is the stereotype skating picture of all time; particularly a Stag Jump Over Mountains! Since I was a little boy I had always wanted a picture of myself doing such a jump, because I had seen a picture of Dick Button, in a Fair Isle sweater, doing one – complete with mountains. It was the ideal of the time.

Actually, all one has to do is jump, and bring one knee up, and there it is, but it looks physically impressive. Eventually I did get my Stag Jump Picture, with a woollen sweater, over the mountains – although they were the Rockies and not the Alps. But never mind. It meant I did not have to do Stag Jumps anymore!

REFLECTIONS INC.

As Mr Mosler is Chairman of the fund-raising section of the United States Olympic Committee, it seemed only right for me to appear in the Benefits which he organised at Madison Square Garden. For my last, after the Olympics, I had a great desire to do something 'different', something which *I* thought might bring a lot of extra people to see the performance. Mr Mosler agreed to the 'something different', and also to my suggestion that we might approach the choreographer Twyla Tharp. At our first meeting, she asked me why I had wanted to meet her, and I told her that it was because she had created the ballet which made the most sense – to me, and about 'me' – on the subject of growing up; what it is like to be young and the problems that attend it. The ballet is called *Douce Coupe*; it is the one that, for me, says so much about how I felt it *should* have been when I was young. Twyla said: 'That's why I made it, because it is exactly the same for me; *I* felt it should have been like that, too.'

After our first meeting, she looked at a lot of films of me skating, and then arranged to watch me practise one day. She said: 'I've got three hours. Show me everything that one can do in skating on the ice.' I began with school figures and worked through, and then I worked through free-skating and the basic elements; then all the most difficult things that we can do, so far. I finished by just skating around. Basically, the plan of *After All* is exactly that: a summary of my talking and demonstrating on that first occasion for, literally, three hours. She hardly said a word at all. When I could think of nothing more to say or do, she said: 'That's very interesting. I'll see you tomorrow morning.'

She came back the next morning and said: 'Oh, I've just been thinking. Would you try this, please?' And she put together a combination of steps that had never been done on the ice before; they were totally new ways of moving on an ice-skate. And they all worked. This floored me; I could not believe anybody could do that. Also, I could not believe that after twenty years I had not thought of it myself! Twyla Tharp, in one day, had gone home, thought about it and understood it, enough to come back and actually devise a whole sequence of steps that had never been performed before.

We worked together for three weeks after that, and we worked very hard. In New York, 'private' ice is very scarce, and we had to go out to New Jersey to practise in a rink there, which meant me leaving the house at six in the morning. I would drive across Central Park, pick up Twyla, and

After All

then we would drive to New Jersey and work until late morning, before driving back into the city again. Her intelligence of approach to the whole thing made the task exceptionally enjoyable in every way. It was also the most challenging thing I had ever had to do, because everything I had learned in the past really did not help me very much.

When Twyla first came to rehearse, she said: 'I must learn to skate.' At that time I needed to go to England for a week, and Twyla said that she would learn to skate during the week I was away! In fact Twyla loved it. Occasionally she would put the boots on and ask me to drag her out and tear around. She liked to go fast, and we would hare around like a couple of lunatics, but she would be the first to say that she has not totally mastered skating yet! She said that she would only take a bow after the performance if she could actually skate on. She *could* skate on and off properly, but she could not master a curtsy on skates. There came a point when I suggested that we were probably spending more time on her 'on and off', and its curtsy, than we were on the rest of the piece! She added the Third Movement only a week before the event; it was not in the original concept. It did make more logic of the piece and finished it off very nicely.

The performance of *After All* was very, very exciting; possibly because of the risk involved. Being in a Gala full of American skaters, who tend to be the most extrovert performers in the world, this piece was so diametrically different that there was no way we could guess, in advance, about its reception. It was not really until the day of the rehearsal, when I watched everybody else practising their pieces (mostly to pop music), that I realised exactly what most people expect of Skating. In a curious way my mind was refreshed by the thought. The other performers watched me rehearse my own item, to Albinoni's Trumpet Concerto in B flat, and some giggled and some were thinking, very obviously: 'This boy's gone *crazy*!' In the evening, 14,000 people came along to the performance; it was, at that time, the largest audience that had ever assembled in the United States to watch figure-skating. A lot of those people were from the Dance world, and had come along specially to see Twyla's new work, because the pre-publicity had been extensive. I do not think I have ever been so nervous in all my life. But in the end they seemed to love it. Everybody stood up to applaud, and Twyla eventually took her curtain call in rubber-soled shoes.

GEORGE KALINSKY

performin 'After All'

Thoughts about presenting

The Theatre of Skating

After the Olympics I met for the first time Larry Parnes, the theatre impresario. He had contacted me as a result of comments I had made in interviews, concerning my desire to see Skating become a form of real Theatre and not remain always at a superficial level. I made no decisions at all as to who might or might not represent me; as an agent or as a manager. It was a time of talking and listening for me. I spent several months travelling around the world, listening to the people who wanted me to do ice-shows, or sign this or that agreement. In a way it was as disturbing to be potentially rich as it had been to be perpetually poor. I found myself worrying for days over the difference between 2·50 million and 2·55 million. Although I had never before been tempted by the ice-shows, there was, at this point, a huge temptation being dangled in front of me. Suddenly I found myself thinking: 'Well, for a year or two it might not be so bad. Of course I could always do what I really *want* to do, *after* that.' Life-time security, in exchange for two years' work, was on offer. There are many people who think, perhaps rightly, that I made a terrible mistake in finally saying 'No' to all this. But I know that I would never have had the energy, or the impetus, to do what *I* wanted, after two years of ice-show touring. To have wasted altogether the opportunity that was already before me, given the fact that I had the mental impetus, and was 'news' (as well as being new on the scene) would have been – to my way of thinking – an even sillier mistake.

So I returned to London for further discussions with Larry Parnes. He and I finally agreed that we would work together for a six-months' trial period, after which we could decide – both he, and I – if we liked the arrangement. The first six months were certainly difficult in terms of reaching some form of common ground or policy. I think that Larry did not really believe how determined I was to put my own ideas to the test, rather than drift back into the well-established pattern of ice-shows, which became a recurring theme in our talks. Because an impresario was now on the end of a telephone, rather than myself, there were, suddenly, better offers for all the shows and touring schemes to which I had already said 'No'. It was depressing to discover how hard it was going to be, to break out from the format that everyone visualised for a skater.

In the summer of 1976 I recorded the television Special for subsequent transmission on Christmas Day of that year, and, travelling back to New York after the recordings were finished, I found myself in the position of having ahead of me no planned work whatsoever. It was a disturbing position to find myself in. It is true that an English impresario had tentative plans to produce my show, but by the time I was back in New York I learned that the backing had been withdrawn and the idea itself dropped.

It was in a mood of frustration and, I suppose, anger, that I put together on paper my ideas for a show that could be creative as well as relatively cheap. From twelve o'clock one night until about four in the morning, I sat making notes. In the morning I put the whole lot in an envelope and posted it to Larry Parnes in England. I gave it very little thought after that, but a few days later, Larry telephoned to say that he thought the show was a good idea, and he suggested that it might be done at the Cambridge Theatre. My initial reaction was that the Cambridge was far too small, but in checking every other theatre in London we discovered that there was nothing else available. So I agreed to try the scheme at the Cambridge, feeling

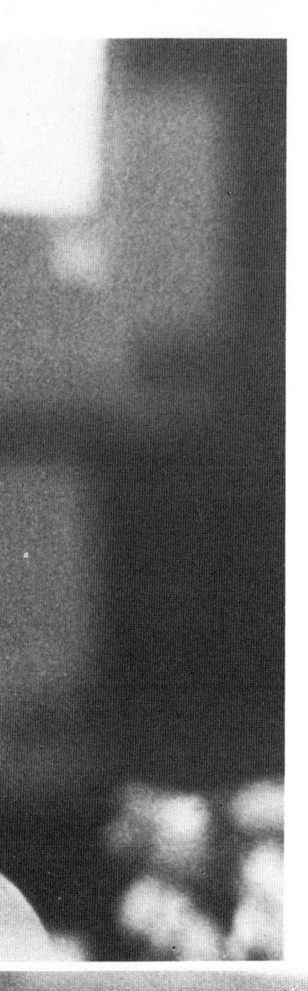

that it would be a good chance to discover, in a relatively inexpensive way, whether the basic concept worked. There were days of general indecision, principally concerning the size of the stage. I marked off an area of ice on the rink in New York. Every day I skated only on this area: the same size as the stage at the Cambridge. Confining myself within this area, I became more and more disheartened and frustrated, but I did discover eventually that if I made certain modifications, then I could do quite a lot on that space. In fact my technique in some things had to be altered radically.

Chatting with Nancy Streeter over tea one day, I came to the conclusion that I should really try, even if the circumstances were not perfect. From that moment on, Larry set the wheels in motion and it all happened very quickly. We were scheduled for a December opening – within two days of the television show being transmitted.

the show gets on – dressing-room preparation for the first Theatre of Skating

Dancing and Skating

If I could turn back the clock, I would be a dancer for one reason. Dancers have a *tradition*, and generations of knowledge and work behind them. It supports them. I know it is a very hard world, as many other worlds are, but at least the supportive background is there for them to lean on if they want to do so. In what I am trying to do, there is nothing for me to lean on. I envy them their chance.

I always knew that I had one thing to say in life, and one thing only: I believe that skating can be expressive. I think it is the only thing I shall ever have to say; but then perhaps there are people who would envy me even that. In terms of Dance, I knew that if I had slogged away for a number of years I had the possibility of becoming a mediocre dancer in the *corps de ballet*, which doubtless I would have enjoyed – I would quite like stomping around with a garland in *The Sleeping Beauty*! But I really felt that Skating gave me the possibility of *saying* something. Rightly or wrongly I plodded on in that area, and now I do have the chance that I wanted. Sometimes I think I have achieved nothing. Sometimes I think I am doing quite well, and that what I hope for is not a fool's dream.

In terms of having other people take the same approach as myself, I often think that as I am so far from 'it' myself, it does not matter if nobody joins me. Then again, I know that if I do not keep plugging away at this particular small endeavour of mine, and I stopped, then it might not be merely the end of me but also the end of anyone else who might otherwise have a go. It might fix a general label: 'This has been tried and it did not really work.' Although I cannot recommend wholeheartedly the life of a skater – in fact I would not recommend it to anyone at all – nevertheless, by the nature of things I might end up teaching people who would ignore that advice; and perhaps I might, just *might*, teach one person to skate beautifully. But it is all such an imponderable. I met someone, at a party, who said to me: 'You can convince me while I can actually see you do it; but the second you go off, I do not believe it any more. I do not think it is possible.' For an uncommitted audience this must always be the case. In any area of theatre one is lucky if, now and again, something touches a chord within one. One is very lucky if that happens at all.

In 1974, after my disastrous World Championships in Munich, I thought seriously about the possibility of giving up skating and trying to get onto the lowest rung of the Dance world in some capacity. I had been offered a scholarship at the Alvin Ailey School of Dance, the direct result of my having taken classes there at the time I was preparing my piece to *The Rite of Spring*. I had decided then that I ought to know just a little – the most basic, rudimentary elements – of what modern dance is all about, and I started taking Graham classes, and also classical classes, at the Alvin Ailey School. I did this for four or five months before I made up the two-minute programme for *Rite*.

I found it all very absorbing, and during Robert Christopher's classical classes I had often talked about the possibility of my becoming a dancer of some sort. I had said to him: 'Do you think there would be any chance of my becoming a dancer – even of very little ability?' And he had thought that there would be, though there would need to be an enormous amount of work put into the change-over. He must have seen that I was prepared to work hard, so the scholarship offer really arose through him. This all happened at the time when I was deciding whether to approach Slavka Kahout, and when the introductions to Gus Lussi and Carlo Fassi eventuated I made the decision to go to them, which effectively ended the possibilities at the Ailey School. Robert Christopher put on a very North Country voice when I told him, and said: 'Ah yes. Go and do it for Queen and Country.'

Getting into one's make-up is, to me, a relaxation before a performance, and more than anything else it is a mental preparation. Ritual would be too strong a word to use in this connection, but it is a form, a series of preparatory exercises. There are numerous things that I tell myself while I am getting ready, and there are images that I often repeat to myself: things that get me into the feeling of doing a certain piece; they are all part of one's warm-up.

I always try and vary my appearance as much as possible between the various rôles, because I am conscious of the fact that the audience has to sit there looking at me in five different works. If I *can* change myself in any physical way for these items, then I will do so. Even facial make-up and hair is changed for each piece. Now, I know all those make-ups very well, and I *feel* that I look different, even if it is not apparent to an audience. Actually, I feel different in myself. In *Valse* I do not care for that person; I think he is rather nasty. He is flippant, and a show-off, and only skin-deep in his feelings, but then that is the way I want him to be.

preparing for 'Valse Glace'

Jazz Suite

The first thing I had to consider for the show was the choice of choreographers. I had already worked with Norman Maen on the London Weekend Television show, and the encounter had been pleasant and successful from my point of view, so he was an obvious choice. Before the TV Special, when we first met at the producer's house, neither of us, I suspect, was particularly impressed with the other. I had been told that Norman Maen wanted to rehearse with me for one day, in London, before I went back to New York. It crossed my mind that this was a strange plan; that whatever we did then, in the Spring, would be forgotten by the Summer. But I duly arrived at a rehearsal room in Soho at ten o'clock one morning. Norman was there, with an assistant to play music. We started, and he set me a few combinations of steps on the floor, and after about twenty minutes, he said: 'It's all right; you can go home now.' I thought: 'This is *very* strange. Maybe this is the way they do it in television.' And I went home feeling rather cheated by the whole thing, having expected to work the whole day and doing, instead, only twenty minutes. He told me later that he only agreed to work with me *after* that; he had wanted to know if I could actually move at all, other than on ice-skates. He had thought it would take him the whole day to find out, but apparently twenty minutes were enough to make him risk it. For those twenty minutes I had been auditioning for my choreographer. It is just as well I did not realise this at the time, because had I done so I am sure I would have failed!

In considering music for the first theatre show, I had to take into account the fact that I could only have a very limited number of musicians, so the Cambridge show was formed with pieces in which solo instruments predominate. As a variation, a jazz combo seemed to me a good idea as a way of introducing something more full-blooded, so Norman Maen was deputed to choose some music. It turned out to be very enjoyable: music by Thad Jones and Mel Lewis, arranged by Dave Lindup. My 'invisible white hat' dance was originally intended to be my only part of it, but then we found another piece of music, called *A Child is Waiting*; with this ballad as the central block we were able to expand the whole thing, and I joined in that too.

My real solo, with the 'hat', was intended as a homage to soft-shoe dancers; there was not intended to be an Astaire connotation. Norman knows that area so thoroughly that he rattled the whole thing off in about fifteen minutes. I loved doing it, but I had never actually seen a soft-shoe shuffle! Despite my ignorance, it was fun for me to do. Most people's impression of me at that time was of someone who skated to *Don Quixote*, looking terribly sad about everything. I was desperate to correct this image, and *Jazz Suite* was ideal, but it took me a long time to get to grips with it, never having had to mime anything before. Norman, and his assistant 'Mo', coached me and worked with me very, very hard on how to 'work' to a camera, and later, how to project to an audience. *Jazz Suite* tumbled out of Norman, and I thought it was a real success; ideal for the whole company.

three different days, four different carousel jumps – the first three pictures taken from a side angle, revealing the actual foot placing; the last from directly in front to show the placing to its best advantage

various angles on a split flip with a twist; pictures taken at the moment of maximum impulsion before a mid-air turn resulting in a backwards landing

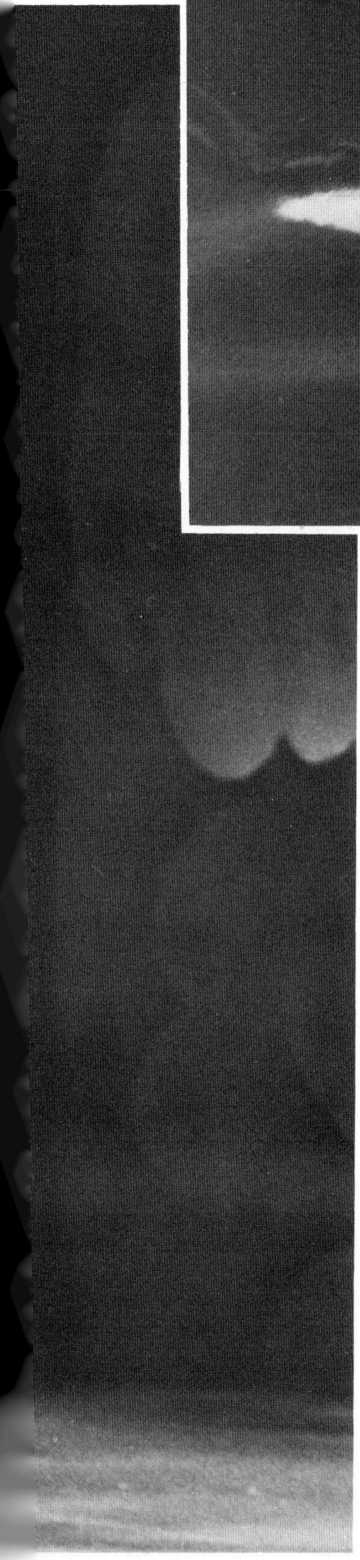

left: skid stop to catch 'the hat'

above: from the white suit to the green, after a rapid change in the wings

inside spread-eagle

different days and different angles on one choreographed leap in 'Jazz Suite'

the company for the first Theatre of Skating, from the left:
Paul Toomey
Lorna Brown
John Curry
Paul McGrath
Jacquie Harbord
Bill Woehrle
Cathy Foulkes

If ever anyone wants to hurt me, they can dismiss my work as being that of a frustrated dancer – and they would be absolutely right. I am. I have always tried not to put ballet steps onto the ice, but sometimes I do things in a balletic way – if I am lucky. I have loved dancing for as long as I can remember.

When I was eighteen, and first came down to London, I heard from friends about a wonderful dance teacher, a lady who taught in Notting Hill Gate. Off I went, to Joyce Graeme, and it was instant adoration on my part. I had never before seen anyone who could move quite like that. Like all wonderfully gifted people, she can make the most simple movement seem fascinating. One watches such people and wonders what it is that they are doing that makes them look so totally different from another person doing basically the same thing alongside. Joyce Graeme confirmed my passion for movement; instilled it in me.

Whenever I was in London from that time on, I kept the ballet classes going; they were the high point of my week. There was novelty in it: the atmosphere was different from the ice-rink, and so were the people. Even to this day, the Ballet world is still a very glamorous and mysterious world as far as I am concerned. Now, when I watch rehearsals of various companies, as I often do, it does

still seem wonderful to me. Perhaps some of them come and watch us, and perhaps it all seems wonderful to them.

At the time my first show was in preparation, I was adamant that the company would take regular ballet classes as a matter of course, and Joyce Graeme was the obvious person to ask for, as Ballet Mistress. She must have thought it curious that the boy with the tin feet was still cluttering up part of her schedule.

Scenes of Childhood

with Lorna Brown

I was delighted when Peter Darrell accepted my invitation to direct the first show. He took some time off from running the Scottish National Ballet, and came down to London to work with us. He had already been over to New York to talk with me, and when I first played the Schumann *Kinderscenen* to him I do not think he was very excited by the general idea, but he went away and re-thought the whole thing, and turned up with a vague story-line which linked the scenes in a very 'misty' way.

Of all the people from the Dance world with whom I have worked, Peter was the most nervous about *skating*; he worried about his lack of knowledge of the technicalities.

Most of the work was choreographed on the floor and then transferred to the ice, which may not be ideal, but at that stage there were endless problems over the ice unit and there was nothing to skate *on*. I think *Scenes of Childhood* was a good piece which suffered from my own insistence on the way the programme was shaped. It was my idea that I should appear first, and that the presentation should be very low-key. I had felt that all the ice-shows I had seen were always structured to give the star a grand entrance, and I had not wanted this approach for myself. I did not realise that by sliding out on the stage first, in the first piece, I was in some way cheating the audience of their chance to say: 'Hooray – here you are! Glad to see you.' By wafting on and doing a very subdued and lyrical piece, I was doing the last thing that anybody expected of me. That was a serious structural fault – and it was *mine*.

slow turns in arabesque

Scenes of Childhood suffered from being first in the programme, with a single piano and quiet music. At that point the audience was still getting over the shock of seeing skaters on a stage at all; taking in such curiosities as the noise of skates on ice. The first piece is the one in which the eye and the mind need to have time to adjust; and in that particular one there was no time for adjustment. I think everyone sat through *Scenes of Childhood* wondering whether or not they were going to like the general idea of skating on a stage, rather than watching the piece itself. Had it come later in the programme it would have made a greater impact by contrast. It has a natural development of theme and character – something entirely new for skaters. I liked doing it because I knew 'who' it was in the piece; I recognised all the growing-up processes that were portrayed.

a forward jeté

two different angles, different days, on a forward edge with a kick position

backwards travelling arabesque on a bent knee, in skating terms known as a grafström; the second picture showing the left leg beginning the preparation for the following movement on that leg

Feux Follets

During a Royal Ballet season in New York I met the director of the company, Kenneth MacMillan, and almost his opening words were to the effect that he liked my work so much that he wanted to choreograph something for me. Of course that was the thing I had most wanted to ask Mr MacMillan, but it would have taken me months to summon up the courage to approach him. When the show was planned for the Cambridge, a MacMillan piece was obviously high on the list of priorities.

Kenneth MacMillan is one of the calmest and most ordered people to work with, as well as being such a pleasant person in himself. He is systematic to a degree. He did say that he wanted to choose his music, and he settled on Liszt: the Study No. 5 in *Feux Follets*, known as 'Will-o'-the-Wisp'. It is one of the hardest pieces of music for a pianist; when one looks at the score there seems hardly any white left on the page. I thought the will-o'-the-wisp was really more of a dragonfly skimming across a pond. There is a poem, with a line that reads: 'All who follow, follow in vain.' This was the thing that I always said to myself before the piece started.

The choreography is incredibly difficult for a skater to perform. When Kenneth MacMillan was setting the work, he would ask me rather anxiously if I thought I was capable of doing the whole thing every day. Because I have a horror

fast-moving spiral, MacMillan style

of ever saying anything is too difficult, I always assured him that I could manage it, but in doing so I set myself the most enormous task; technically it is something of a killer. I only started to get anything like correct in it towards the end of the run. From a skater's point of view, *Feux Follets* is an amazing test of control; it is difficult to know what an audience's point of view would be, but I loved doing it because it was challenging. It gave me something to worry about every night. In rehearsal I got to be very good at it, but I never liked doing it in a costume which seemed to leave me too 'naked' as a skating body. I did it badly on the opening night. Much later, the piece got back to what it was supposed to be, but I still could not 'hide' in the costume. That made it even more diffcult. I want to do the work again; on a bigger stage and in a different costume.

I think the first real ballet that I saw was the Royal Ballet Touring Company, when it came to Birmingham. There was one ballet which I saw over and over again because it was so often in the repertoire at that time. It was called *House of Birds* and I did not approve of it at all – the girls never wore proper ballet skirts! Wherever I went – Birmingham, Leamington or Coventry – to see the ballet, they were always doing the bird one, and I was always disappointed because there were no white dresses. If the girls were not wearing tutus, then I considered that I had not seen a proper ballet. I suppose the movement kept my interest, nevertheless.

Although I have never been influenced by the style of another skater, I have often been asked if I have modelled myself on any noted male dancer. I have not, if only for the fact that I was not sufficiently aware of any of the gifted ones until after my own approach had set. If I had had any sense, I might have sought out these people; might have pursued performances by Nureyev or Dowell or Wall, but I did not. The only thing that did make a definite impact on me was the uniform tastefulness of performances by The Royal Ballet; all its dancers have this very controlled, very English, beautifully stated way of doing things. My test for myself was

*eft: the landing moment
f a 'flying camel' (a parallel
ump ending in arabesque turns)*

always: '*If* The Royal Ballet were to see this, what would they think of it?' This thought even governed my choice of musical snippets when I was an amateur; certain conjunctions would have seemed 'nasty' to The Royal Ballet, with the result that I avoided doing something like putting Mozart with Mahler. The Royal Ballet, as a whole, became the invisible arbiter of taste, governing my own views on music, and even on costume. Their overriding taste was an influence on me, rather than any individuals as such.

The person whose performances I have most admired, and the person who above all I would always choose to see, given such a chance, is Fonteyn. Of all her infinite qualities, one feels most that while she is dancing, she can hear more of the music than one can oneself. I have derived more enjoyment from watching her than I have from anything else in any area that I can think of. On top of all this, she is also a great *star* as such, which adds to the excitement.

Valse Glace

so I turned to Drigo's *Le Reveil de Flore*. Poor Ronnie did not care too much for this lightweight choice, which seemed a bit like sugar with sugar on top, but we desperately needed a traditional showcase opener, where we could do some 'whizz-dashery', which everyone loves to see in skating.

Having seen several of Ronald Hynd's ballets, I knew that he had a wonderful feeling for dance as *theatre*, quite apart from the excellent choreography. I felt that criticisms of my first show had been justified. It certainly worried me that the show had been described as humourless, and I did hope that Ronald would correct this failing in some way. With that in mind, I put Gilbert and Sullivan in front of him, as well as Drigo. I had felt that a lot of the people who came to the first show, came because they wanted to see something similar to that which I had done at the Olympics, and at the Cambridge that need was not satisfied.

We required a piece that would allow me to do all the fireworks and skating tricks in a bright, non-serious showcase. I decided that Anna Pavlova was quite cunning when she chose some of her music,

the classic sit spin

Although I do feel the chap in *Valse Glace* (as the Drigo piece came to be known) is a bit of a flash cad, I enjoy the rôle and its moments for showing off! It is all very Ruritanian and jolly, so that I do not worry about the difficult technicalities that are incorporated into it. It is fun to do.

with Jacquie Harbord

When Ronald finally tackled the task and we got to the end, where there is a great swoon in the music, I was very alarmed that he might want to do that bit as a *pas de deux*. So I claimed it firmly, saying I wanted that bit for *myself*, with the whole rink and the chance to swoop around it. I knew that it was traditionally the moment for the lady to come on in the ballet and do all her balances, but I was unrepentant; I wanted it!

There are very few *adagio* dances for men in ballet, which I feel is a pity. The current male solo in the first act of the Royal Ballet *Swan Lake* is a good exception, and it helps the whole story; and in *Dances at a Gathering* there are lyrical moments for men; moments that are wistful. But there seems, on the whole, a convention that men should not tackle *adagio*.

To have music always seemed the most natural thing to me. Even as a small child, if there was no music playing when I was on the rink I would go to the sound-system lady and say: Would you please put some music on?' To this day I dislike practising in a quiet ice-rink; I always put something on. Except when I am doing school figures; then music drives me crazy. But for most of the time I must have music, otherwise there seems no reason for moving at all.

Visually, I was enormously impressed by the few people I had seen who were real experts, like Jacqueline du Bief. She wrote a book about skating, called *Thin Ice*, and it is really the best book about being a skater that has ever been written. She was full of magic and had marvellous ways; and the sort of ice-shows they did then, like *Peter Pan* or *Snow White* were, I thought, fantastic. They kept to the story, absolutely straight, like a real pantomime.

nowadays. I find this deeply upsetting, because they would not be seeing the magic of that woman as an entertainer. In that final ten minutes in the shop window, with no music that I could hear, she was able to inspire and enchant, and that is what it is all about. For her day, Sonja Henie was a technical genius; for our day she would be far from that – she could not begin to do some of the jumps that people do today. But conversely, most people today could not begin to capture any of her kind of feeling or spirit. This is a great pity. Now it is all so technical; everything boils down to how many 'hoops' one can jump through.

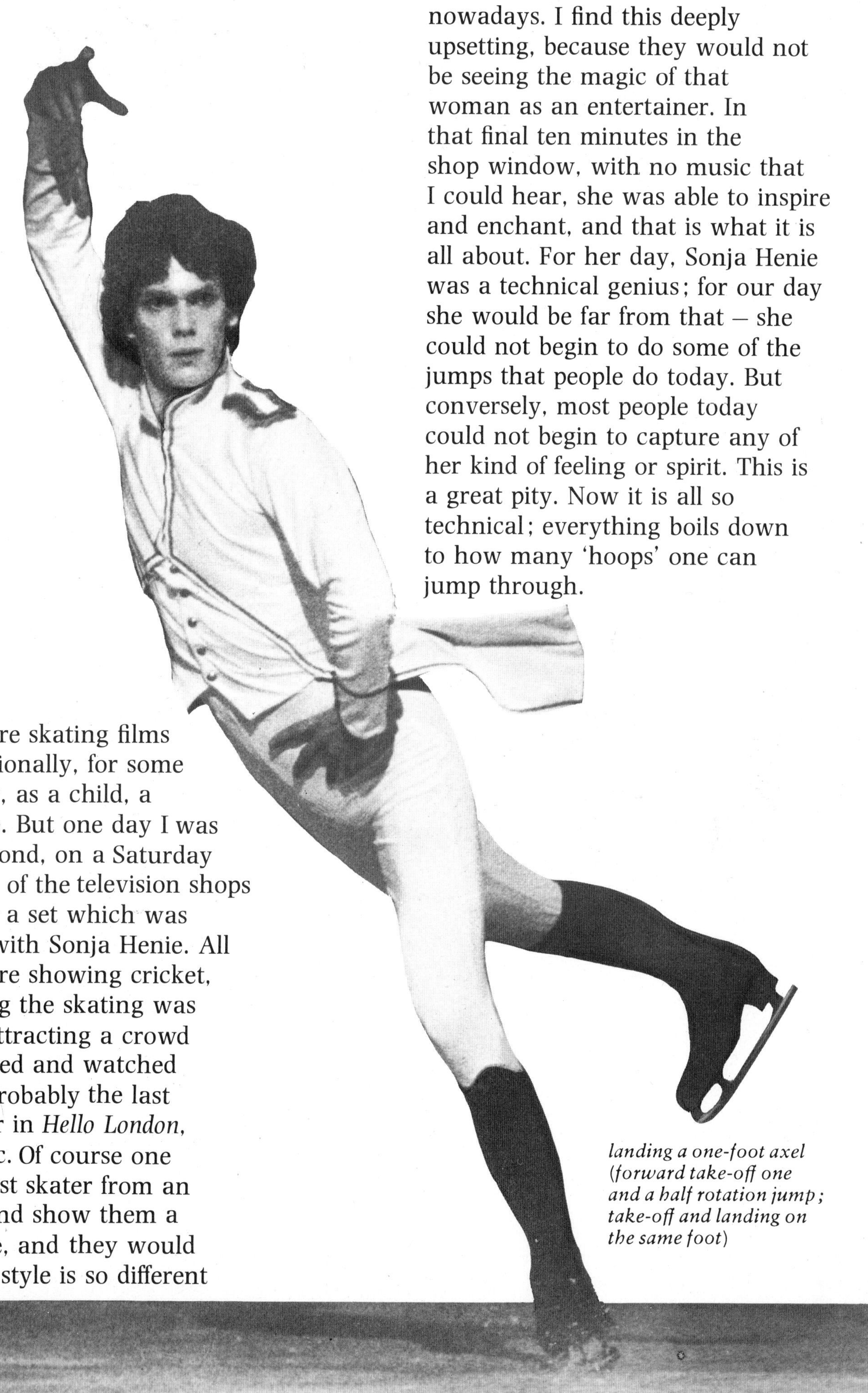

landing a one-foot axel (forward take-off one and a half rotation jump; take-off and landing on the same foot)

Although there were skating films on television occasionally, for some reason I never saw, as a child, a film of Sonja Henie. But one day I was shopping in Richmond, on a Saturday afternoon, and one of the television shops had in the window a set which was tuned in to a film with Sonja Henie. All the other shops were showing cricket, and the set showing the skating was the only one not attracting a crowd of onlookers. I stayed and watched what I *think* was probably the last production number in *Hello London*, and she was terrific. Of course one could take the worst skater from an ice-rink of today, and show them a film of Sonja Henie, and they would laugh because the style is so different

Winter 1895

Although I had been given permission by Sir Frederick Ashton to re-mount his ballet *Les Patineurs* for my own programme, reluctantly I had to drop the idea because I could not increase the number of performers to accommodate it. In the end I thought it would be nice if we had our own skating party, even though we had a smaller cast, and I suggested Gilbert and Sullivan to Ronald Hynd, who chose the Sullivan music he thought most suitable. We were thus walking a tightrope between *Les Patineurs* and *Pineapple Poll*, but we needed an ensemble piece that was light and amusing, and in the end Ronald produced something that seems to have its own distinct personality.

I must confess to being extremely shy about doing my own part in it! It was Nadine Baylis' idea to make me a Cockney Pearly Prince, and she really had to push me into the rôle. I did not mind being a newspaper-seller, but I wanted to be an *ordinary* one, not a Pearly Prince; however, Nadine thought it would be good for me to do something totally out of character, so the pearl buttons were stitched on by the dozen. At first it made me blush every time I did it; belting around and skating 'rough' was

obviously not my forte. Clicking my heels and doing 'incorrect' things, I used to think: 'Oh dear – Mr Vickers would not approve of all *this*!'

left: the Cockney Pearly Prince, with Lorna Brown as the toffee-apple seller

bottom: the company for the second Theatre of Skating, from the left:
David Barker
Linda Davis
Marc Battersby
Yvonne Cameron
Angela Greenhow
Timothy Welch (ASM for the company)
John Curry
Cathy Foulkes
Ron Alexander
Robert Metcalf
Lorna Brown
Jacquie Harbord
Paul Toomey

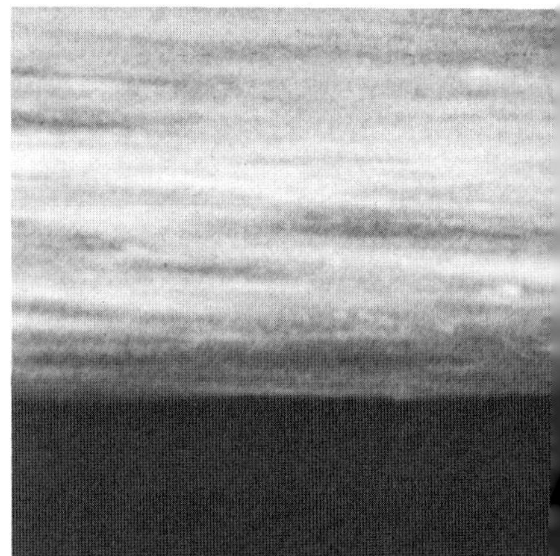

Winter 1895 has come to be great fun for me, and I do think it is the perfect type of work for an entire company to perform. The piece owes its name to the fact that we discovered that there had been a very severe freeze in 1895 and every class of society probably would have ventured onto the ice during that time.

L'Apres-midi d'un Faune

with Cathy Foulkes

Faun was something that I had wanted to do for a long time. I thought that the wonderfully sustained *legato* quality was ideal for a skating interpretation, and the haunting and mysterious essence in the music had always appealed to me, but I had never used it because I could not contemplate the idea of severing any part from the whole.

When the chance came to incorporate the whole score in the television programme, there was some concern as to whether an eleven-minute piece would sustain itself on commercial television. I was convinced that it could, and Norman began choreographing the

piece for myself and Peggy Fleming. Having thought about the piece for so long, there were, rather naturally, a great many things that I had envisaged for myself. Although Norman's viewpoint was very properly a different one, I liked immediately what I was given to do; it came up very easily, in fact. As far as I was concerned, it was the most successful part of the television show.

Because I could not have a full orchestra for the first theatre show, initially I intended to discard *Faun*, but in the course of preparation for the season at the Cambridge, one of the pieces was cut, and we needed an extra item to replace it. I taught *Faun* to Cathy Foulkes in one afternoon, to the piano transcription. We had to adapt certain parts due to the increased *tempi* of the piano, which cannot sustain musical lines in quite the same way as an orchestra, but it worked out well.

For *Faun*, I used the costume which had been made for the television show, in that first theatre season. In a sense it coloured my initial reading of the rôle. I had said that I wanted the work to follow the original concept of the faun and the nymph, but to be slightly more modern in feeling, not purely classical. I wanted it more animal than human; not like the boy and the girl in the Jerome Robbins version. Although I love that version, I wanted, for myself, to try it in a more animal-esque way, but in the trouser costume I found the

human element remained uppermost. When Nadine Baylis came to design the second Theatre of Skating show she had, of necessity, to include *Faun*, and she found a very clever way of disguising the boots and allowing me to have a more traditional costume for the piece. Immediately I wore it, I felt the 'animal' emerge in me.

As I came back through the curtain one evening, I caught sight of myself in a piece of mirror, and I realised then how near Nadine had managed to come to the 'feel' of the original Bakst/Nijinsky image. I had read the books about Nijinsky, and his own Diaries, and the many accounts of that ballet. Even though I have never seen the Rambert version, I still have a feeling that I know exactly what

that original Nijinsky ballet looked like. Even the stories surrounding the making of the piece leave one with a hundred images; one recalls all the people involved, and how much of a radical departure it had seemed at the time. It always interested me that Debussy is supposed to have disliked the choreography because he felt it matched neither the set nor the music; that he felt the music was fluid and round and the choreography was static and angular. For myself I was absolutely intent about two points in the score; that at those moments we should stand totally still. I think they are probably the same points where Nijinsky stood still. To me, the music *insists* at that point that one do nothing.

Originally, Norman wanted me to begin the piece in a reclining pose, on a ramp, but I felt very uncomfortable about the idea. I did it a few times in rehearsal, and then one day Norman said: 'Why don't you start it standing up?' So I heaved a sigh of relief and improvised the beginning as it is now. We never changed it; it

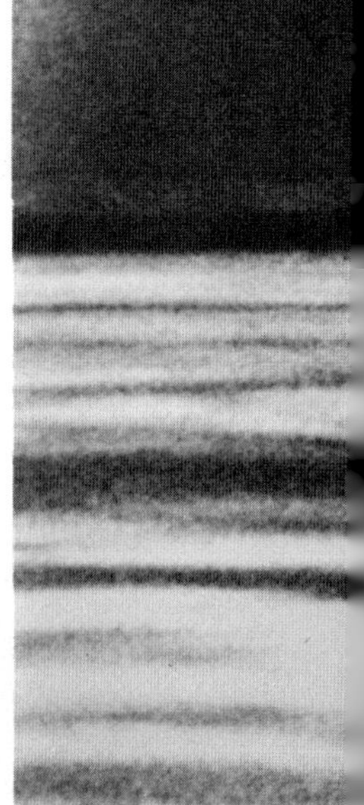

seemed to be all right. In the double work, because of Peggy's pregnancy, the lifts were designed to be very simple; it was the first time I had done any partnering where real feeling was called for between partners. I think *Faun* is the most satisfying of the works I have done; I enjoy it the most.

with Cathy Foulkes

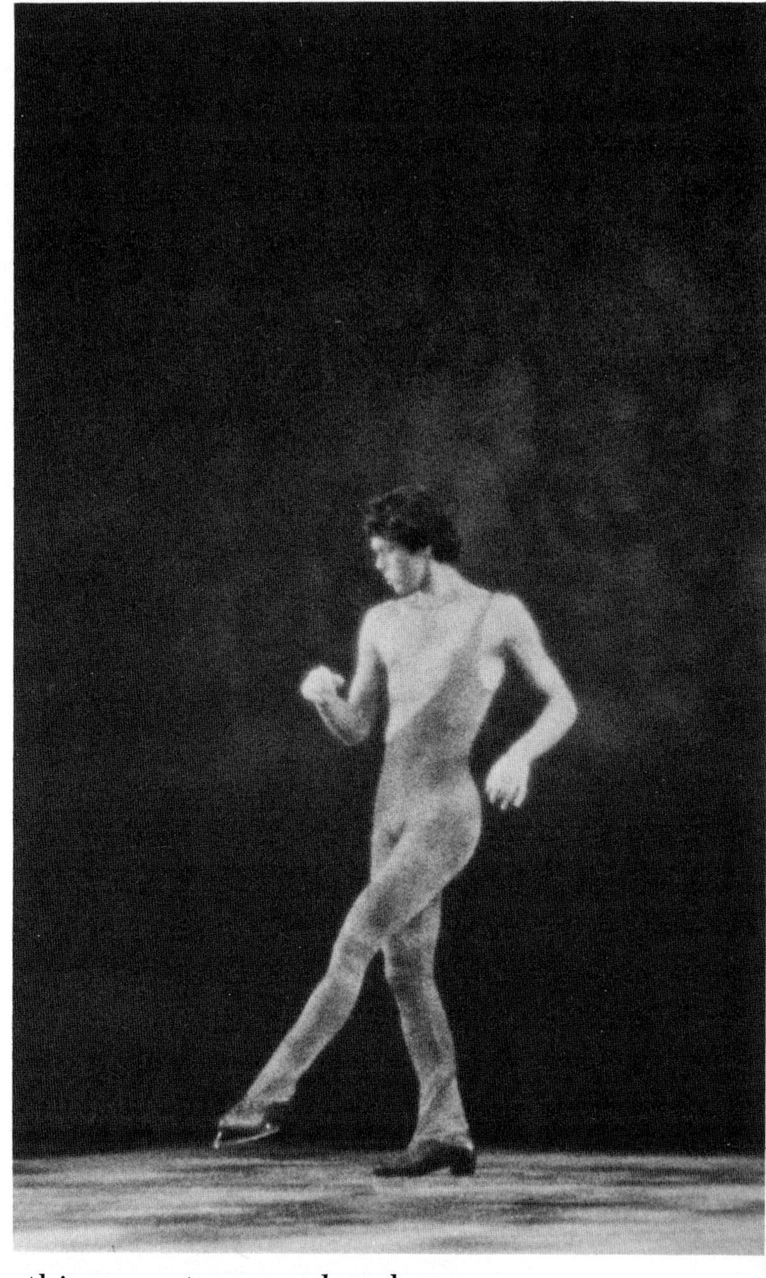

There are few times when I feel that it does not 'work' for me personally, and I would have to be in a very tired and exhausted state for it not to mean something very special to me. It sometimes surprises me how alien I look when I put the make-up on, which is a direct copy of the Troubridge portrait bust of Nijinsky in his make-up for the role. One reads how it took him hours to do, and how nobody spoke to him during that time, and all this sometimes crosses my mind when I am getting ready for *Faun*. In both shows I have had a matter of only a few minutes to get into the whole thing; costume *and* make-up; during which time I am trying to think, hopefully, about what I am about to do. At the Cambridge I had literally to run down the stairs to make the entrance in time, and as I clattered down I used to laugh to myself and think: 'It was never like this for Nijinsky!'

On stage, I do find that I am 'in' the piece rather deeply, to the extent that I can sometimes 'see' the trees. I make myself see them. They are always the same trees; *English* ones, actually. I often wonder whether an audience thinks anything is odd, when I am looking around a 'tree'. Of course, there are none on the stage for the audience. But as for me, I can barely see any of the sky for the leaves and branches. And the girl is a figment of the imagination; to me she does not really exist. At the point where we cross downstage it is as if I go through her and come out the other side, and she disappears from my mind.

It is a purely personal interpretation that the faun is real but that the nymph is not; that he has been merely dreaming about her. The most important thing is the sun, coming through the big chestnut leaves. There are other parts where I 'hear' things in the woods! For instance, where there is the 'ting' of a triangle, the instrumentation seems, to me, to be the snapping of a twig. I *do* think about these things, and it is almost embarrassing to reveal the fact. But in *Faun* everything does seem real, because the music means so much to me; everything about it is close to me. As a piece of music it has sustained me at difficult moments in my life. I do not know whether it is a good or bad thing, identifying so closely with one piece of music, but with *Faun* that is the way it is.

were there to be only one photograph of myself skating, the one on the right is the one I would choose, because the image I see on the paper corresponds exactly with the image in my mind at that particular moment

Among the people with whom I discussed items for the second show was John Butler who – of the choreographers I have encountered so far – was the only one with actual experience of working with skaters. At the time of doing his early ballet work he had also done shows in America for skaters such as Dick Button. Although John was prepared to do an ice ballet for me, initially he could not think of a theme; he knew only that he wanted it to have some form of dramatic narrative. As I had always thought that the element of flight could be transmuted into skating better than in dancing, I suggested the legend of Icarus, and John thought the subject had possibilities.

As we discussed it in New York, he became more and more intrigued by the idea, but the actual creation of the work proved a precarious struggle. As with all shows, the budget had been set at a certain figure, and in the usual way this had gone way over. It was at this point that most people seemed in favour of cutting the *Icarus* project. I was so determined that we should do *Icarus* that I ended up having to commission it myself; there was no possibility of us having it otherwise.

Icarus

with John Butler

John arrived from America to start work. It was not easy. We were preparing five new pieces and re-mounting two, with what was basically a new company. The time pressures were great, and it fell upon me to be involved in nearly all of this work in one capacity or another; either through learning three new pieces, choreographing two others, or rehearsing the remainder. My concentration and effort were spread over a very large area, and John is – naturally – used to working with people who have only one principal project on hand at any one time. While I never gave anything less than my total energy to *Icarus* whenever I was working on it, I did also have to give my total energy to other things, at other times of the day. As always, there was too much to do and not enough time to do it in. We spent much of the first week simply learning a style of movement that John wanted, and he recorded each of these progressions on

the final stage rehearsal of a new leap devised by John Butler (see preceding page also); the jump analysed and refined by reference to the video recording. The flash on the screen shows the moment when the photograph on page 197 was exposed

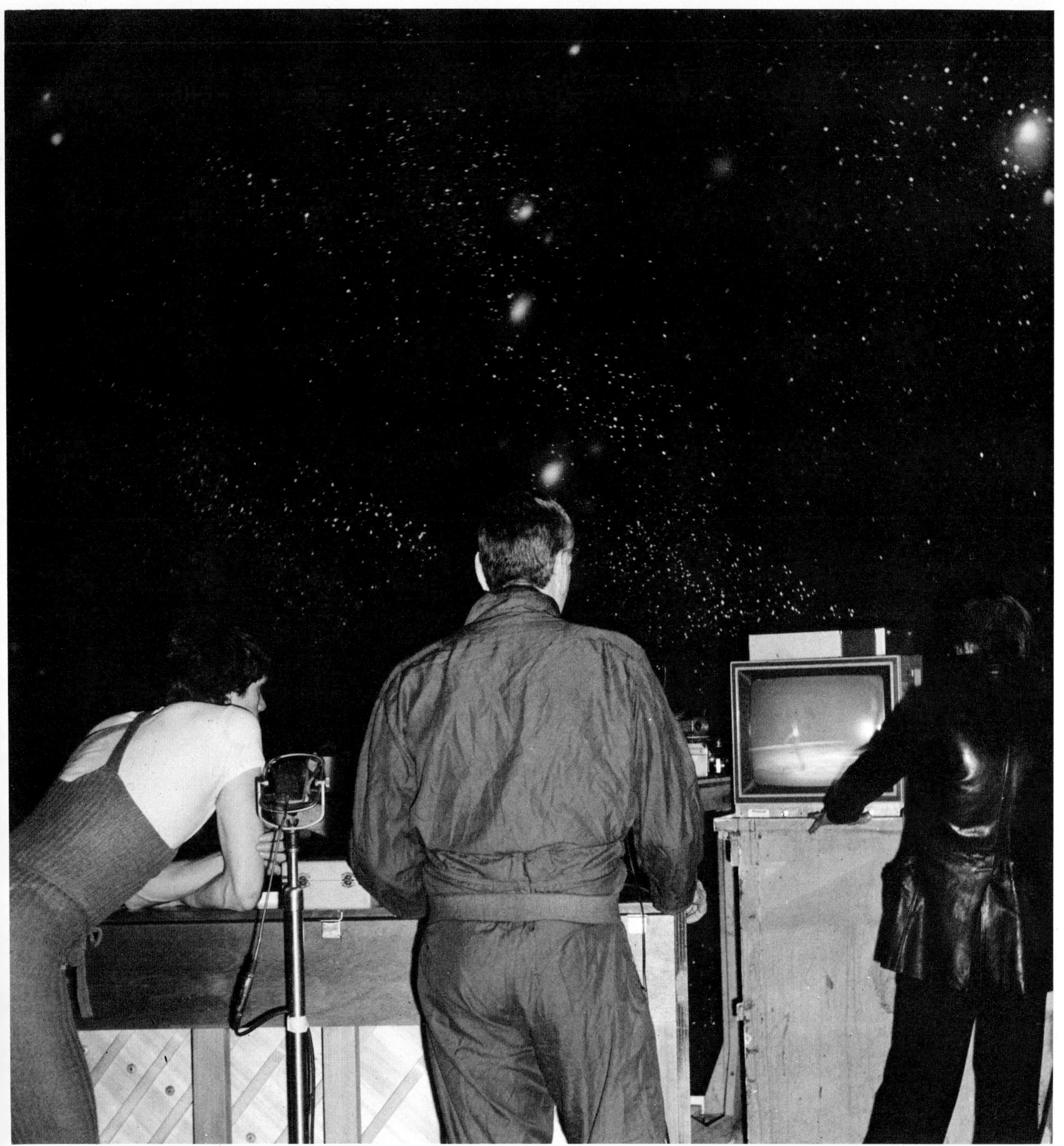

videotape, so that nothing would be lost and we would have a reference-file to draw upon. In this way we acquired many more than we used. John used the video to point out elements that he was looking for; I might do something four or five times and then we would view the tape and he would say: 'Look – *that* one! You did it *there*!' He was looking for an extra dimension, or dynamic, and for a performer there is nothing to compare with a visual lesson. I think videotapes are awful; I hate them for what they reveal. Awful! But they have their uses.

with Nadine Baylis busy working out the Icarus costume (of chamois leather) on a real live dummy!

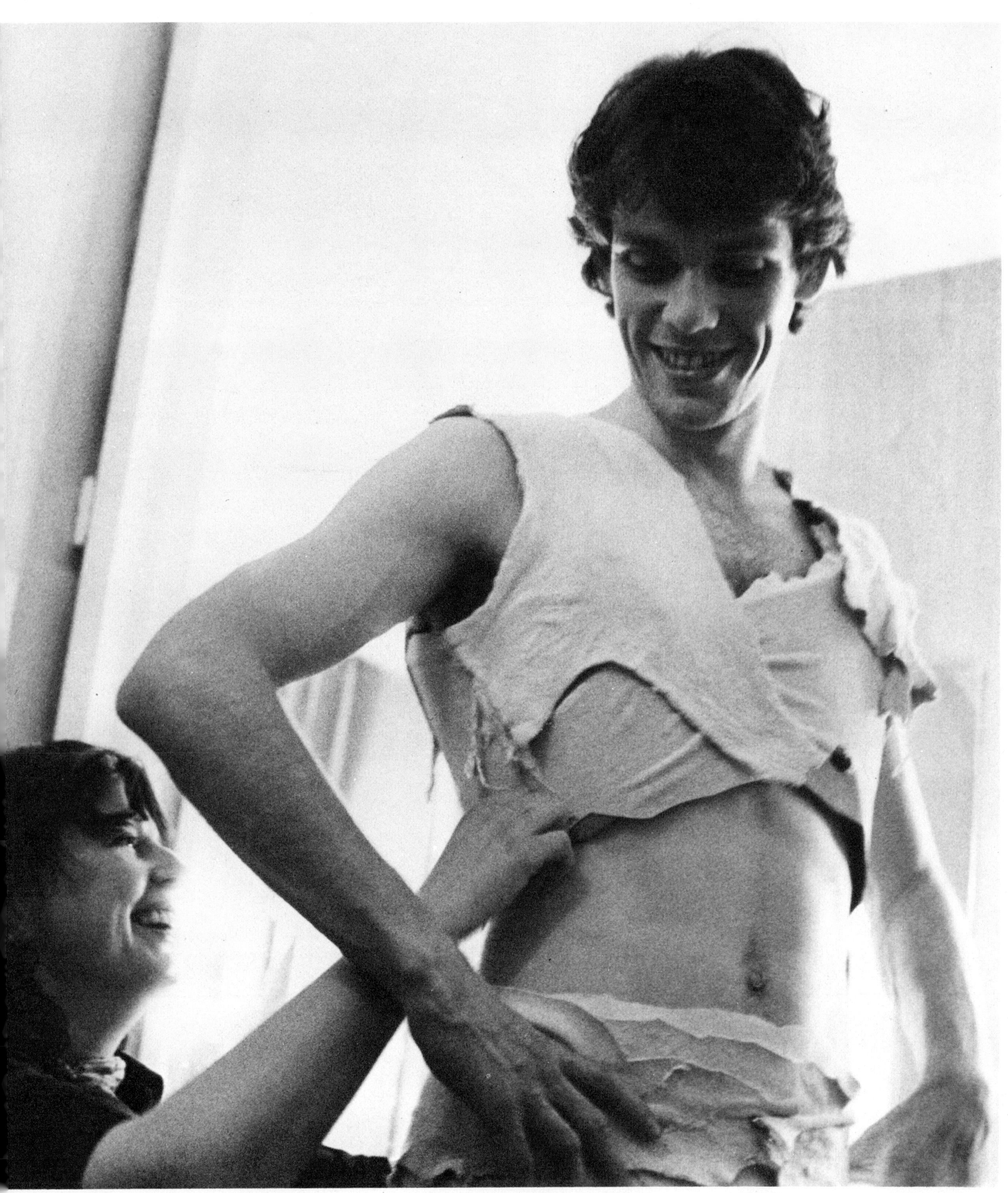

episodes such as costume fittings often provide amusing interludes which break the more serious and energetic aspects of rehearsal

We had problems with John's choice of music, which could not be played by the relatively limited number of orchestral players at our command, so we had to commission a new piece of music. We were rather tense waiting for the outcome, but Gordon Cross composed a new score in a matter of days, and it proved to be marvellous when finally we heard it played. There was, too, worry about my being lifted and thrown about; I am not the world's bravest pairs-skater. I would rather be the thrower than the throwee! I even found time to worry about the costume, which seemed to cover very little of me. But we progressed. Nadine produced a huge silk cloak for my first entrance, and we all liked the drama of it. There were also the wings, which I used initially without their silk panels – just the framework. When it came to the final rehearsals with the wings in their finished form, I found the wind-resistance extraordinary; so tiring and restricting that I felt as if I could hardly move. Despite all the problems, John's construction steadily emerged, and as a work I feel it is very much the direction in which I personally wish to go. I think it does break new ground.

in rehearsal, with Ron Alexander as Daedalus

with Ron Alexander

Originally, we intended a skater to take the rôle of the sun, but finally settled for Daedalus and Icarus, with the sun as a huge stage prop.

There are many things in it which are very difficult, and fraught with a certain amount of risk. There are jumps at strange angles, and I spend much of the last part spinning around with my back bent over while I look upwards. John was perfectly aware that he was structuring entirely new things; he wanted to invent new jumps, and design movements which we did not think would, necessarily, work – until we tried them. Although one is scared, one is also excited by such departures. When we came to do the two weeks in Bristol, as a run-in for the Palladium opening, it was very clear that *Icarus* was the least well-received of any piece on the programme. On some days there were actually boos and hisses while the piece was in progress. In London, the reverse was true; it seemed the most popular item in the entire show, and certainly the critics devoted much of their space to it and were enthusiastic about it.

John Butler is a very intense worker, and his intensity shows in the piece. When I skate *Icarus* well, I myself feel that kind of intensity.

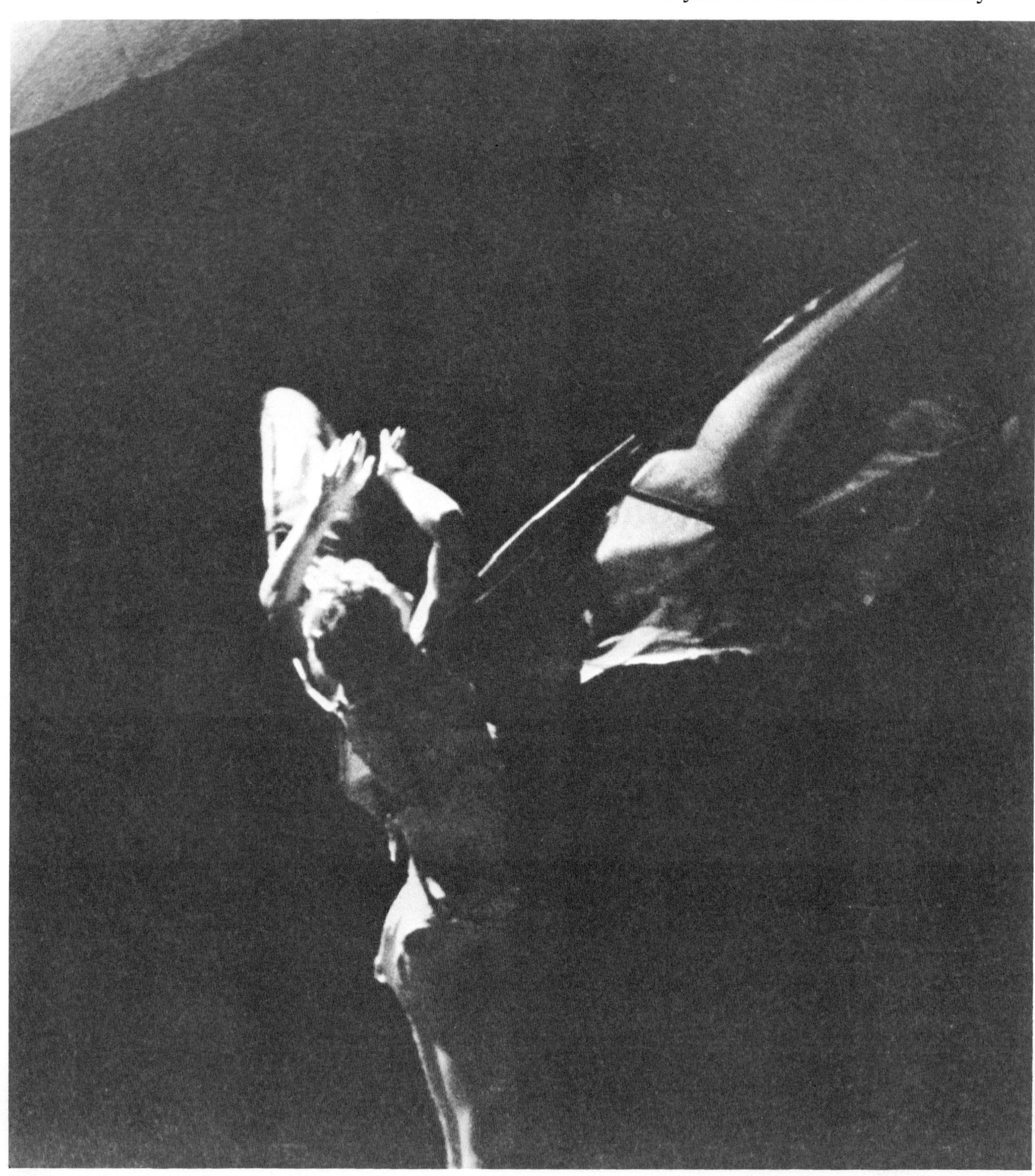

One of my beliefs has always been that *everyone* wants to fly too close to the sun; wants to get to something very badly; and when they do get there, they usually find that the thing they want – whether it is the sun, or whatever golden object one might think of – is their ultimate undoing. That theme was more important to me than anything else.

BILL AND NELLA STONE

One learns from people all the time by absorption; one learns simply because one is there watching, or listening. Two people can do something within a given framework, and the activity of one can come over as being a very emotional and involving experience, and that of the other can come over as being an extremely difficult exercise. Sometimes one understands why certain things 'work', and why other things do not; one assimilates by preference.

There are only certain times in my life when I feel any kind of real unity or completeness or peace: these times are when I am skating. The ice, then, is home.

I do not know what to think about my work. I am very grateful when something I do brings someone pleasure; I think this is the best bonus one could possibly have, though I have to be honest and admit that giving other people pleasure is not the motivating force for doing it. I do not accept such an idea. I skate because I love skating myself. Certainly I would like to think that, one day, there might be half a dozen companies like mine, each working away and producing interesting results. But then that would make me slightly bitter; I would be too old to go around as Guest Artist!